COSGROVE

PORTRAIT OF A LEADER

PATRICK LINDSAY

RANDOM HOUSE AUSTRALIA

Random House Australia Pty Ltd
20 Alfred Street, Milsons Point, NSW 2061
http://www.randomhouse.com.au

Sydney New York Toronto
London Auckland Johannesburg

First published by Random House Australia 2006

National Library of Australia
Cataloguing-in-Publication Entry

Lindsay, Patrick.
Cosgrove : portrait of a leader.

Bibliography.
Includes index.

ISBN 978 1 74166 528 4.

ISBN 1 74166 528 0.

1. Cosgrove, Peter, 1947– . 2. Generals – Australia –
Biography. I. Title.

355.0092

Cover photograph © Newpix
Back cover photograph courtesy of Graham Dugdale
Typeset in 13/17 Bembo by Midland Typesetters, Australia
Printed and bound by Griffin Press, South Australia

10 9 8 7 6 5 4 3 2 1

CONTENTS

Acknowledgements   ix
Introduction   xi

1   Sunray Two-Two   1
2   Early Days   33
3   The Flying Cosgroves   49
4   Cadet Cosgrove   61
5   The Greasy Pole   83
6   The Lion of Timor   111
7   The Chief   149
8   Back to War   169
9   The Collins Affair   187
10 The Final Salute   207
11 The Art of Leadership   225
12 Reflections   243

Glossary   253
Timeline   256
List of Illustrations   262
Bibliography   268
Index   279

To Lisa, Nathan, Kate and Sarah
. . . inspirations all

ACKNOWLEDGEMENTS

My sincere thanks to all those who helped to shine light on Peter Cosgrove's life.

My special thanks to Mike and Jo McDermott.

To Jeanne Ryckmans, Catherine Hill, Jody Lee and all the team at Random House, my thanks and admiration for your outstanding professionalism.

To Lisa, for her unswerving support and love.

INTRODUCTION

He inspired us by his simplicity, his own rugged type of down-to-earth approach to men and events, his complete naturalness and his absolutely genuine humour. He was a great leader – true; he was a great commander – true; but to us he was, above all, the well-loved friend of the family.

British soldier and historian Lieutenant General Sir Geoffrey Evans wrote these words in his biography on the great British World War II commander, Field Marshal Sir William Slim. They could just as accurately be applied to General Peter Cosgrove.

They say that a country gets the politicians and the army it deserves. And that may be so. But, while those living in democracies have some control over the political leaders they elect, they have no such control over their military leaders. That we have produced a warrior and a leader of the calibre of Peter Cosgrove should give us great pride. He has proved himself in battle. But, greater than that, he has shown himself to possess all the characteristics we admire in our diggers: courage, coolness, audacity, endurance, devotion, ingenuity and, perhaps even more importantly, compassion, loyalty, larrikinism and humour.

Peter Cosgrove is in many ways an Australian Everyman: a knockabout character who loves nothing better than a good yarn over a beer, yet an unassuming but inspirational leader.

He began his career as Staff Cadet 2342, Cosgrove P. J., in January 1965 and retired with honour in July 2005 as 235341, General Peter John Cosgrove, Chief of the Australian Defence Force. In between, he gave Australia 40 years of dedicated service and left the ADF as our most respected and best-loved general in living memory.

Like most Australians, I first saw the man they call Cos when he stepped on to the world stage to brilliantly lead the INTERFET peacekeeping force in East Timor. Like most Australians, I wanted to know more about him. He graciously agreed to launch two of my books, *The Spirit of Kokoda* and *The Spirit of the Digger*. But it wasn't until I began this book that I fully appreciated the depth of his character and the ways he has affected the lives of so many.

Cosgrove: Portrait of a Leader is the result of a fascinating journey discovering the man under the slouch hat. I hope it does him justice.

SUNRAY
TWO-TWO

1

★

**Operation Jack, near diggers' rest fire
support patrol base,
Phuoc Tuy Province, South Vietnam,
October 1969**

'Two-Zero Alpha . . . This is Two-Two. Contact! Wait
Out!'

'I say again, Two-Two Contact! Wait Out!'

Garry Mayer just managed to spit the words into the
handset of his field radio to alert company headquarters
to the firefight before he dumped his pack, grabbed
his rifle and radio, and raced after his young platoon
commander who was fast disappearing around the
corner of a bamboo thicket.

Private Garry Mayer was only 22 and a National Serviceman but he was already an old hand in Vietnam-combat terms, having been more or less continually on operations for ten months. His unit, 9th Battalion Royal Australian Regiment (9RAR), was unique. It had been raised from scratch by its Commanding Officer (CO), Lieutenant Colonel Alby Morrison, who'd been given just one year to man, train and deploy the battalion on active service to Vietnam. He started at Woodside in Adelaide on 13 November 1967 and, as ordered, the 800-strong battalion left Port Adelaide on the 'Vung Tau Ferry', the troop carrier HMAS *Sydney*, on 9 November 1968, bound for Saigon's Vung Tau Harbour.

In the intervening 12 months, Alby Morrison had assembled the unit's officers, non-commissioned officers (NCOs) and diggers in Woodside and then overseen their training in Cultana and Leigh Creek in South Australia, the Land Warfare Centre at Canungra and finally at Shoalwater Bay in Queensland. From the time it arrived in Vietnam, 9RAR was almost continually on operations. In its 12 months and 23 days of war service, it was operational for 325 days – 80 per cent of them 'beyond the wire' or outside their fire bases.

Garry Mayer's new platoon commander officer was also 22. Lieutenant Peter Cosgrove had graduated from the Royal Military College, Duntroon, less than a year earlier. He'd joined 5 Platoon B Company 9RAR as a 'reo' (reinforcement) during their previous operation and had only been in-country for about a month, after a short stint in Malaysia.

I was on the steepest learning curve imaginable. Leaving Duntroon as one of its less promising graduates, about halfway up the class, I think I probably had some strengths which suited me for infantry: I was a pretty determined player of sport, a knockabout sort of a figure, not afraid of hard work or the sort of privations of infantry life, so I would have carried that with me but into a totally unknown environment.

Cos had only been in Vietnam for about a week when he got his first confirmation of the perils surrounding him. He was on mine warfare training prior to being assigned to his platoon command when Mike McDermott, his closest friend from Duntroon, also in Nui Dat training prior to assignment, arrived unannounced. Mike told Cos that he'd just heard a radio report that a young Duntroon officer had been killed while serving with the SAS. He'd parachuted out of the back of a Hercules at 2000 feet, collided with another soldier and their chutes had 'candle-sticked' (entwined and failed to open).

Cos and I knew who it had to be – a mate who'd graduated with us, Charlie Eiler. We went off and had a cup of coffee and sat down and talked about Charlie for a while. He was the first bloke we knew who was killed. It was a real shock to me and to Cos too. And we thought, Well, this is what happens . . . It happened to a lot of our friends.

Cos had little time to digest the tragic news before he found himself in a chopper skimming over the lush paddy fields near the town of Dat Do to take command of 5 Platoon who were already in the bush on Operation Neppabunna. It was late August 1969 and the first thing that struck him when he met his men was their 'thousand-yard stare', the haggard, war-weary look in the eyes of combat veterans. Another characteristic of the soldier in the field hit him; the smell of men who'd been wearing the same sweat-saturated clothes for weeks in the jungle. He immediately liked their bearing, just as he thought he would after he'd earlier caught a glimpse of their brand of humour, illustrated by the sign that welcomed him at the entrance to their base camp which read: 'The Fornicating Fifth, 5Pl B Coy. Let others panic . . . We refuse!'

Cos had come to Vietnam confident in his ability as a soldier. He felt he was as prepared as he could be to lead men in battle, in theory. Like men through the ages, deep in his inner core he harboured a nagging doubt about how he would handle himself under fire, in what soldiers call 'the fog of war', that terrifying, confusing, concussive, swirling and disorienting heat of battle.

I was very lucky, I had a bit of an apprenticeship as a young commander with a quite experienced and polyglot lot of soldiers in 1RAR in Malaysia where I was a team commander for four or five months effectively, before going off to Vietnam. So I was technically not too bad and I'd also had this experience with good NCOs helping me, sort of training me before I took over this bunch of hard cases in Vietnam.

But Cos knew how he would have looked to his new charges, as he wrote in an army newsletter years later: 'I did my best to look focused and cool (although I had eyes on me like a mad cat and the brain was whirring at 10,000 rpm).'

Like all soldiers faced with a new commander – especially a reo – the diggers of 5 Platoon B Company 9RAR were watching Peter Cosgrove like hawks.

You learn all kinds of things, you learn a lot about yourself because the diggers mirror in their own reactions how you're performing and perhaps the strengths and flaws of your own character. All of these guys had been there a while, and there was a trickle flow of reinforcements coming in and old hands moving on but the nucleus of this mob had been together since before the battalion went on operations. I was lucky again to have good NCOs. The team was well trained. Their discipline and jungle skills were all good. They were quite confident in each other. They just had to find me out.

Cos was well aware of his men's ambivalence towards him. Years of listening to his dad and his grandad, both career soldiers, and his formal army training had prepared him for the fact that respect did not automatically come with his appointment as platoon commander. He knew he would have to earn that respect, by his actions not his words. He found it easy to talk with his men and to make decisions and to give orders – he always had – but he tried to curb his natural enthusiasm and his desire to jump into things full-on until he felt he'd earned his men's trust.

> I suppose I held back a little, simply so that I wouldn't offend by coming on too strong, not in terms of the decisions but in terms of establishing rapport. That was probably reasonable. I joined them while they were on an operation that, while it was exciting across the board for many parts of the battalion, was fairly routine for my platoon. Apart from me being an enthusiastic executor of the tasks given to me by my boss, the fundamental questions of 'How's this guy going to go when we get into battle?' were still unanswered.

So far, 5 Platoon liked what they saw of Cos. He was solid, in stature and demeanour, and he was approachable. On patrol, he seemed to know his stuff. He was confident in his decision-making skills and keen to take on the enemy. To a seasoned soldier, this could be a two-edged sword. An inexperienced officer could be a danger in action, particularly one who was trying to impress. Garry and the other diggers from 5 Platoon had already endured some harrowing experiences. Early in their tour of duty, they'd been caught in an ambush in a minefield. Johnny Hallam, a fine digger, had lost his legs. Another digger, George Nagle, and one of their most experienced corporals, Midge Graham, had been killed and half a dozen others had been wounded. It was a shocking introduction to the realities of war for Garry Mayer.

Midge was an older soldier, a really good soldier. His death hit us hard. I was sharing Midge's tent and I had to pack all his gear up. The day after he was killed, his wife committed suicide.

The diggers of 5 Platoon had gone through a lot together; in many ways they'd grown up together. Most had joined the unit around the same time and then trained as a team. All their partners knew each other. Like most units, they were a tight group. In Vietnam, after nine months on almost constant active service, they'd become mentally tough and physically hardened. They routinely carried gear on patrol that weighed more than 45 kilograms. Despite the energy-sapping heat, many erred on the conservative side when it came to carrying ammunition. Machine-gunners were supposed to carry 150 rounds of ammunition but many carried 500 rounds or more. Most carried eight 1-litre water bottles – two days' supply – in addition to grenades, claymore mines and M-72 rocket launchers. Their outdated World War II-issue packs had been replaced with new versions that had an easy-release system that allowed them to pull two tags and dump their packs when they had to move quickly into action; something Garry Mayer had to do when he bolted after his new boss.

After 5 Platoon's earlier losses, their previous commander, Lieutenant Ivan Clark, had led them well, always aware of the constant dangers surrounding them. The last thing they needed was a gung-ho reo. The platoon were on the second phase of Operation Neppabunna, where their main job was to protect land-clearing teams that were cutting back bush and jungle areas, getting rid of the cover to the Vietcong. The swampy land in which they were working bogged down many of the clearing team's heavy graders and their work disturbed some very angry boa constrictor pythons. They killed one during clearing and it provided a much-welcomed delicacy for some local villagers but it put the diggers on edge as they kept a keen lookout for its mates. During the work, four Vietnamese children had blundered on to a mine near the Australian base and had been killed. It was typical of many similar soul-destroying incidents that characterised the war, and it badly affected the men who had to secure the area and recover the children's bodies.

Towards the end of the operation, 5 Platoon had been moved by armoured personnel carriers further north where they'd found and destroyed an area of Vietcong food crops. With his men, Cos had watched as one of the neighbouring units was involved in a fire fight. Their company commander, Captain Graham Dugdale, had called in 'Spooky' – a Hercules aircraft specially fitted with three 7.62 mm Gatling machine guns, each capable of firing 6000 rounds a minute, which produced a devastating concentration of firepower and dealt with the opposition. It was a sobering glimpse of the real thing. Cos had taken control with a sure hand but he and his men knew that he still hadn't experienced his baptism of fire.

On 30 September, 5 Platoon were airlifted by chopper to Diggers' Rest Fire Support Patrol Base, about halfway between Nui Dat and Bien Hoa, where they began a month-long series of patrols called Operation Jack. It was what they called a 'reconnaissance-in-force' by the battalion and it had two main aims: one, to find and destroy any enemy forces in their area of operations and, two, to protect the US Army's 60th Engineer Company, a land-clearing team ordered to destroy thousands of hectares of vegetation in the Hat Dich area, north-west of Nui Dat. The area had been the subject of many previous aerial defoliation drops, known as 'trail dust' missions. Little did they know about the long-term impact of the insidious chemical sprays, including Agent Orange, which was dropped on and around them. What they did know was that they were operating in an area known to include some Vietcong Main Force units, the best-trained and most experienced of the Vietcong forces.

Just before last light on 30 September, B Company, which included 5 Platoon, moved north-east out from Diggers' Rest and began protecting the land-clearing teams by constantly patrolling ahead of the clearing.

During this time, Garry Mayer was able to observe

Cos at close quarters. Garry was originally an M-60 machine-gunner in 5 Platoon. He'd injured his shoulder in an inter-company rugby match and after he recovered he'd been assigned as the platoon's signaller in charge of the radio. He formed part of the platoon's headquarters, along with Cos, his sergeant and their medic. He'd eaten with Cos and chatted at length with him, and discovered that they both loved their rugby and sport. He was impressed with Cos' ability to speak on a wide range of subjects and to communicate easily with his men. He admired the way he was able to retain the common touch without losing his authority. Garry also noticed Cos' attention to detail and he recognised the pent-up energy of a man determined to make a good fist of his job.

On 10 October, 5 Platoon's forward scouts noticed some tell-tale signs as they silently bush-bashed through the jungle; the Australians never used tracks when on patrol because of the danger of mines and ambushes. The signs soon began to add up. Recently used tracks, cut tree trunks camouflaged with mud and grass and the area itself, which featured large clumps of thick bamboo near a stream. It was classic Vietcong bunker territory. The Vietcong constructed a vast array of brilliantly concealed underground camps and conducted a classic guerrilla war from them. Some of these camps were small food or weapons stores or hideaways for locally based troops. Others were large subterranean towns, including field hospitals, barracks and kitchens, with labyrinths of inter-connecting tunnels and caverns. They were usually booby-trapped and contained a variety of escape exits.

The Vietcong generally preferred to avoid pitched battles, unless they had an overwhelming superiority in numbers.

Cos and his men were on full alert when they caught the distinctive smell of their enemy. Some vets remember it as a mixture of 'muskiness, mildew and cheap soap' combined with the effects of a restricted diet of rice, flavoured with fish sauce and vegetable oil. Often this smell was detected just as the enemy opened fire. This time Cos and his men were lucky. They knew they were near a large enemy bunker system and that it was occupied. Cos ordered Garry to call in the find to Graham Dugdale, their company commander. The call came back that Dugdale wanted to speak to 'Sunray'. ('Sunray' was the radio call sign of the commander on the spot. The call-sign system was simple. The first call-sign number related to the company: A Company was 'One'; B Company was 'Two', etcetera. The second number referred to the platoon in each company. A Company had the first three Platoons: 1, 2 and 3. B Company had the next three: 4, 5 and 6. So, as 5 Platoon was number two platoon in number two company, it's call sign was 'Two-Two' and its commander, Cos, was 'Sunray Two-Two'.)

The usual procedure, when a company found an enemy bunker system or camp, was for the first platoon to halt in front of it while the next platoon moved around to the left of it and the third moved to the right. The company commander would call in artillery fire on the bunkers before the diggers moved in for the attack.

11

On this occasion, Sunray Two-Two was told to hold his platoon's advance while headquarters made sure that the US land-clearing team wasn't too close to the action. While they waited, Cos placed one section (of nine men) to guard the main track and moved his other two sections to support it. He positioned a machine-gun crew facing up the track and a sentry ahead of them to give early warning of any approaching enemy. Then they silently waited for permission to continue. Suddenly, shots rang out and Cos bolted off in the direction of the firing.

Garry Mayer remembers feeling a wave of relief wash over him as he rushed to catch up to Cos during that first contact. He was relieved at Cos' instinctive reaction to run to the source of the danger rather than hesitate or to freeze. By the time Garry Mayer reached him, Cos was blazing away with his M-16 Armalite rifle at movement in the jungle to their front. Cos recalled it vividly:

The shots rang out from the sentry and I rushed forward to the machine-gunner about the same time that he was zooming back in. As soon as he was safe with us, we fired into the area. Then one of my corporals said, 'I've closed up on the left!' That snapped me back to reality and I said, 'Good, we'll do the sweep from the left.' The ground looked fine on the left so that's where we went in from and I did the officer thing. I suppose there were five seconds or so when I was shooting like a soldier would be shooting, instead of thinking like an officer would be thinking. There are times when you think and times when you shoot.

In rugby parlance Cos had made his first tackle of the game. His confidence was buoyed, his adrenalin was flowing.

I can remember that the medic was giving me an idiot grin as we were moving through on what was called the sweep. It's when you've fired at the enemy who've fired at you and you start to advance on them. You call it the sweep but actually it's an attack and I noticed that this guy was glancing across at me. Afterwards I said to him, 'What were you grinning about?' It was pure relief on his part because I was doing my job. Strangely, not for one instant did I think I couldn't possibly do that. I remember when the first shots rang out, it came naturally.

What Cos realised later was that they were almost on top of the bunker system and three enemy soldiers had either smelt the Australians or heard their movement through the bush and had come sneaking out of their camp along the same track to check them out. Cos' sentry had spotted them, fired at them and bolted back. Cos and his men swept the area and trapped the enemy soldiers. They killed two and sent one fleeing, clearly wounded.

There was no mucking around, 'Oh dear, oh dear, what should I do?' sort of thing. I was very lucky the training kicked in – all the drills you do, all the fellows were raring to go – so I didn't have to argue the toss with anybody or make an intricate one-hour plan.

It was quite plain that we'd been shooting in this particular area at people who'd been shooting back, this is in deep jungle, so we just did a left hook with one of the sections and I went with the section and we killed some enemy in that battle. We'd resolved the danger to ourselves very emphatically and I'd answered some questions from myself. I'd also answered some questions on my platoon's behalf, I guess.

The Australians located the bunker system, stormed it and captured it. The enemy adopted its familiar tactics and withdrew. Most of the Vietcong vanished deeper into the bush to fight another day. The bunkers surrendered considerable intelligence, from captured documents together with food supplies and arms. For Cos, the action was a turning point.

I went from not having a clue of what combat's like to saying, 'Well, that's what it's like', and the transition was instantaneous. I suppose I'd been carrying around a certain sense of anxious expectation from when I was warned I'd be going to Vietnam . . . I knew I was going in as a reinforcement and that I'd go on to be an infantry platoon commander there.

Probably from that time there was this sense of anxious anticipation or expectation. When I think back, it probably reflected itself in checking things all the time and being almost paranoid about the accuracy of navigation and that sort of thing. All the things, where, when and if the moment arrives you want to make sure that you've done all you can in preparation.

From that day, for the next three weeks, the platoon was in combat almost every second day. Cos thrived on the adrenalin. His only concern was preventing his men from suffering battle fatigue. He felt the heavy weight of his responsibility for their safety.

I was always aware that every platoon gets a little battle weary, especially if they've seen soldiers who were comrades being carted off, wounded progressively during the year or dead, and it can be exacerbated if a new boy comes in full of enthusiasm.

I felt sorry that they had to break in a new officer where their anxieties were heightened by the fact that I had in my hands and in my brain, so to speak, the authority and opportunity to put them in much more danger than was reasonable. I could do so by getting it wrong, that's obvious, I could even do so by being very right but being very aggressive.

I look back on that and I think that perhaps I was inclined to be right and aggressive – to do all the right things but to say okay we've been given a mission to march to that area, that's where we're going. And when we get there if I look around and it looks like the enemy's been in this area then I'll set an ambush, and tomorrow when we've finished that ambush I'll go for another look around and find another place and we'll put in another ambush.

It was in these early days that Cos' keenness almost cost him dearly. He'd positioned his platoon for an ambush and as they waited, he inexplicably wandered forward to check things out. One of his sentries, Ivan Stephenson, saw movement and was about to fire when he caught a glimpse of a familiar figure. Stephenson was quoted in 2002 in an article by Garry Linnell in the *Good Weekend* magazine: 'We nearly ambushed and shot him. He went very, very close. He was with two others. He was never told about that. If I hadn't looked again, I reckon he would have worn it.'

★ ★ ★

On 16 October, 5 Platoon came across another bunker system. They had noticed movement around the area. It was down by a creek. Their training worked like clock-work. They reconnoitred the position without alerting the enemy. Cos calculated that they faced a force about the same size as his platoon, about 30. Knowing he had the advantage of complete surprise, he silently deployed his troops and attacked. Caught unawares, the enemy fled, leaving extensive supplies of food and equipment.

Headquarters ordered Cos to secure the position and supported 5 Platoon with B Company's two other platoons, 4 and 6, in case the enemy tried to return. The following day, Cos ordered his sergeant to arrange for a water party to go down to the creek to replenish the platoon's water supplies, a constant necessity to keep dehydration at bay. Shortly afterwards, when Cos checked his defensive perimeter, he discovered that, due to a misunderstanding, an entire section had gone to fill the water bottles instead of a few diggers from each section. That meant there was a gaping hole in his defences. He was concerned but he figured the enemy was unlikely to return any time soon and, in any case, his men wouldn't be gone for long. Around that time, his company commander, Captain Graham Dugdale, arrived to confer with Cos. He remembers that Cos greeted him holding his Armalite rifle and ushered him into his platoon headquarters. Graham was bemused at how intent Cos was on engaging him in earnest con-versation rather than letting him wander about the position.

While they were chatting, a couple of the water party were returning when they stumbled across some Vietcong soldiers coming back to their base unaware that it had been captured. The diggers opened fire. The instant Cos heard the shots, he knew what had happened. He jumped up mid-sentence and charged off towards the shots. Once again, Garry Mayer grabbed his rifle and radio and flew after him.

> Cos ran past me, like a bull to a red flag, straight past me, down to where the action was. And I thought, here we go again! But I was lucky that time, my radio was out of my pack, so I could just pick up my radio and go, instead of trying to dump my bag.

Determined to plug the defensive hole, Cos exploded out of the cover and startled the enemy soldiers. He shot two at close range and sent the other running headlong into the thick jungle. Unfortunately, in his dash to the scene, Cos had forgotten to take extra magazines of ammunition. He coolly called to one of the diggers, who'd by now joined him, to toss over a new mag. He jammed it into his rifle and sent the rest of the Vietcong fleeing.

Years later, Brian Vickery, then a captain with 9RAR, realised he'd been visiting B Company headquarters when Cos' action happened.

> I was paying my respects to Graham Dugdale and as I had to wait for a couple of hours before the helicopters would return to take me back to base, I decided to pay Cos a visit in the forward area.
>
> As I was only on a visit, I carried only a 9mm pistol thinking that this would be sufficient as I would not be going far from Company HQ.

I found Cos and we shared coffee and I was just about to leave when the firing started. Cos, as was his style, moved instantly. Grabbing his rifle, he ran at full speed towards the firing and his forward troops. I was somewhat red-faced as I had no real weaponry and very little protection and all the troops between myself and company headquarters were 'standing to' which meant that I could be in real trouble getting back to the helicopter if they didn't recognise me.

So I had to wait for the action to run its course and eventually I had to leave before Cos returned to our location. It didn't occur to me until now that that was the time that Cos earned his Military Cross (MC).

When Graham Dugdale returned from Operation Jack, he reported back on Cos' bravery and recommended him for an award.

I went up to the second-in-command of the battalion and I said, 'Look, I don't know what the criteria are for awards, but Peter's done this and this and this. And he said, 'Oh, it's too late, all the awards have been submitted.' And I said, 'Well since when did bravery depend on a time frame, or courage depend on a time frame?'

Soon after, 9RAR's CO, Lieutenant Colonel Alby Morrison, called Graham Dugdale in to discuss Cos'

actions and asked Graham to submit a report. Alby took
it from there. The recommendation would later read:

> On 10 October 1969, Lieutenant Cosgrove was
> commanding 5 Platoon, B Company. The platoon
> located an occupied bunker system in an area
> where, because of the proximity of allied troops,
> indirect fire support was difficult to obtain. In
> spite of this, he led his platoon in an assault on the
> bunkers without indirect fire support, capturing
> the system and killing and wounding at least four
> enemy without sustaining any casualties.
>
> On 16 October 1969, 5 Platoon located
> another bunker system occupied by about a platoon
> of enemy. Lieutenant Cosgrove silently deployed
> his own platoon for an attack. His assault
> completely surprised the enemy, causing them to
> flee, abandoning large quantities of food, stores
> and documents.
>
> The following day in the same bunker system
> a party of enemy approached his right forward
> section and was engage by the sentry. Knowing
> that the remainder of the section was elsewhere
> on other tasks, Lieutenant Cosgrove ran to the
> contact area and personally conducted the fight
> against the enemy. As a result of his actions, two
> enemy were killed and three weapons and four
> packs containing rice were captured.
>
> On every occasion, Lieutenant Cosgrove
> has shown determination, aggressiveness and

outstanding courage. His actions have been an inspiration to his platoon and company, and accord with the highest traditions of the Australian Army.

Cos knew nothing of the recommendation at the time. He did know a lot more about being a soldier in the fog of battle, as he later recalled:

Battle is terrifying. You vacillate somewhere between sort of a garrulous nervousness through to dry-mouth silence. Your heart is thumping and you're keenly conscious of everything that is happening around you. Your senses are enormously heightened. Your adrenalin is coursing through the veins. You would see people, your friends, dying around you and in some cases you might try to help them, in other cases simply you'd move on, you'd have to move on.

On 31 October, Cos returned by chopper to Phu My, then by Caribou and Chinook helicopter to Luscombe Field airstrip and finally by truck to 9RAR's base camp at Nui Dat.

'The Dat' was home to 5 Platoon and, at that time, some 5000 other soldiers. It was a massive military base, which had grown from its establishment in 1966 as a tiny encampment on a low hill near the main road that bisected Phuoc Tuy Province north–south to a massive military base with a defoliated barbed wire perimeter extending

12 kilometres. It was a buzzing temporary town, alive with movement and noise: from the airstrip and constant transport; from the distant echoes of artillery and mortar fire; and from the radios and stereos of its inhabitants who sheltered from the incessant heat and burning sun in their tents or in the shade of the clumps of rubber trees around the camp. B Company's lines were neatly laid out on the north-eastern corner of the battalion perimeter and had their own showers, latrines, Q store, canteen, kitchen and recreation room. The other company areas ringed battalion headquarters and the helicopter pad, an array of administration and support buildings, the aid post and an open space known as the apple orchard where the diggers watched movies at night. It was a haven from the stresses of operations and it provided a chance for contact with loved ones back home. Many families and sweethearts sent cassettes as well as letters and photos and they were the highlight of most diggers' weeks. Nothing lifted morale like mail from home.

The first thing the diggers longed for when they returned from operations was a long, warm, refreshing shower to remove the caked camouflage cream and dirt, and attend to the ever-present skin irritations and foot and crotch rot caused by the heat and humidity. The diggers tolerated their purple daubs of gentian violet lotion knowing it would ultimately bring relief from the maddening itches. There was also the simple pleasure of pulling on freshly cleaned jungle-green uniforms and dry socks and boots and heading off to the company canteen for a VB or a 'goffa' (a soft drink).

Cos easily slipped into the routine at The Dat. Perimeter patrols at first light to deter Vietcong infiltration, the daily flag raising, 'paludrine parades' where the troops took their anti-malarial medicine, breakfast, inspections, briefings, assignments. He was an enthusiastic supporter of the recreation rooms and the wet canteen and matched the best of them at telling yarns around the barbecue in the evening. He came to appreciate the infantryman's disdain for what they called 'pogos' (officially, 'personnel on garrison operations'). To the infantry, out there in harm's way every day, the people 'in the rear with the gear' lived a far more secure and comfortable life, while they took all the risks. The Yanks had a far less elegant name for them – 'remfs' for 'rear-echelon mother-f★★★ers'. Cos soon realised that the definition of a pogo lay in the eye of the beholder; to the forward scout, the most exposed man in the patrol, everyone behind him was a pogo!

One of the features of a tour of duty in Vietnam was its finite duration. Australia's previous wars had been open-ended commitments but a tour of Vietnam was for 12 months. Naturally, once a digger had passed halfway in his tour, he started counting down the days before he could return home. Most units had a chalkboard counter noting the number of days left: as in '100 days and a wakey' (or wake-up call). By the time 5 Platoon returned from Operation Jack they had less than a month to go. It was to be their last major operation but the battalion continued to patrol in its area of responsibility from Nui Dat and it was on constant call, at 15 minutes' notice, day or night, to act as the ready reaction force to answer any emergency.

In the final days as the battalion prepared to return home, the advance party of its replacement, 8RAR, arrived and its officers were briefed by their 9RAR counterparts. Some officers shared their tents with the men they would replace. Officers' tents were reasonably spacious, 11 feet by 11 feet (3.3 metres by 3.3 metres), protected by sandbags piled about waist-high around the outside. Officers slept on a canvas folding cot-bed.

Just three days before the battalion was due to ship out, the unit was rocked to its foundations.

★ ★ ★

Cos was woken by an explosion. Instantly alert, he realised it was inside the camp. He grabbed his weapon and rushed outside. He knew it came from his right, somewhere near 6 Platoon's lines. When he reached them, he saw smoke rising through a big blast hole in the roof of Bob Convery's tent. Bob was the commander of 6 Platoon, Cos' counterpart. Looking inside, Cos saw that Bob was dead. He'd taken the full blast of a grenade. He was lying in his bed, facing the sandbagged side of his tent. The sandbags had contained the blast and forced it through the roof. Amazingly, the 8RAR officer who had been sharing Bob's tent was unharmed. Cos realised Bob's death was almost certainly murder. It was an extremely rare occurrence in the Australian Army but it was so common in the US forces that they even had a nickname for it, fragging – because the act was often committed using a fragmentation grenade. (In 1969 there were 96 fragging murders in the US Forces in Vietnam. The following year the figure doubled to 203.)

Cos posted a guard to watch over the body and got the other officer out of the tent. He roused Graham Dugdale, who ordered Cos to confine the other soldiers to their tents while he notified the CO, Alby Morrison. Morrison called in the Military Police and they ordered Graham to secure the camp and keep everyone in bed.

The following morning, while out in the field on operation, Cos' friend Mike McDermott received a devastating message.

> I thought it was Cos who'd been killed. I was given a message in the field, from Murray Blake who was my company commander. He said, Hello, Sunray, a person the same level as you, which was lieutenant, from Call sign 2, which was B Company, of the Woodside field, which was 9RAR's base, has been murdered by his soldiers. First letter of his last name is C for Charlie. I sat around shattered for a couple of days thinking Cos had been killed. I found out later the C stood for Convery, poor Bob Convery.

At 9RAR's base camp the morning after the murder, the Provos (military police) began interviewing each member of B Company. They conducted the interviews in a large grassy area underneath the trees opposite the company's camp in full view of the waiting diggers so all could see that there was no coercion. As they eliminated suspects, they allowed them to return to their tents. When they had spoken to each soldier, the police started a second series of interviews and eliminated more. They had begun their third series when one of the privates, Peter Allen, admitted that he'd simply crept up on the sleeping officer, pulled the pin from an M26 grenade and dropped it into Convery's bed before running back to his tent. Allen was arrested and held in an isolated tent surrounded by a barbed-wire fence. Alby Morrison called Graham Dugdale over.

> Alby said to me, 'Righto, you go and tell him he's been charged with murder. You tell him that it's beyond your jurisdiction and we're remanding him for a court martial.' Then I had to go down with the legal officer to identify Bob's body. He took charge of the body and he flew it out to Vung Tau where they did the autopsy. It knocked the hell out of morale.

Cos was pulled out of the field to serve as a witness and sent to a secure area down at Vung Tau where Allen was tried by court martial. He was convicted of murder and the Judge Advocate sentenced him to life. It was difficult to establish his motivation for murdering his platoon commander. Former comrades came up with a variety of possibilities: that Allen's grievances with Bob Convery went back years; that he blamed Bob for some slight or treatment while on patrol; that Allen had recently started taking mind-altering drugs; or that the accumulated stresses created by a year's exposure to combat triggered a psychological collapse.

Whatever its root cause, the episode rocked the battalion to its core. The brief notation in the battalion history speaks volumes. 'The unit's achievements were soured and pride tarnished by the death of Lt Robert Convery, OC 6Pl B Coy.'

The incident ran counter to every tenet of the digger and it deeply affected Cos. He didn't get to know Bob well but it was the first time he'd seen a comrade's body and it reinforced war's random craziness. It also highlighted the consequences of the breakdown of a soldier's discipline and the impact that had on the unit's *esprit de corps*. Cos reflected on the unnecessary waste of a young man's life. Bob was just shy of his twenty-third birthday.

When 9RAR returned home Cos was posted to another platoon based at Nui Dat Headquarters and served out the rest of his 12-month tour of duty with it. It was during this time that he was involved in a number of incidents that persuaded him to temper his enthusiasm in combat. Throughout his later career he would often cite one incident as providing a particularly valuable lesson.

Out on patrol, Cos was dissatisfied with the pace being set by the platoon's forward scout, who was being very cautious because he knew the area was potentially dangerous. Cos took decisive action. He pulled the forward scout back into the main body of the platoon and then stomped up front and took over the forward scout's role himself. Not long afterward, the diggers following him heard a burst of fire. When they reached him they found him standing over a dead bush turkey. A wizened digger turned to Cos. 'Fair enough, Skip . . . now why don't you fuck off down the back where you should be and do your job and let us do ours!'

Later, he learned another lesson that he would carry with him throughout his career.

I did my year in Vietnam and, of course, later in my year I was at the same stage as the young diggers of 5 Platoon were when I took them over. But it seemed to me that I was always pretty energetic and focused. I always felt that I didn't want to entertain the remotest whiff of slackness because I knew that the moment you take your eye off the ball that's when you get hurt. I remember late in my tour when I was commanding a different platoon I suffered the only casualties that my various platoons suffered while I was their boss.

I sent out a half platoon patrol to check on a particular area. To get to where I wanted them to do the job involved passing down what you might call a geographic jug point, a tall hill with a spur line leading off it, a brief flat part and then a swamp, and the swamp was on the edge of a little canal where sampans and native fishing boats plied their trade.

It seemed to me that this little flat part was a

good spot to get ambushed. So I said to the fellow I put in charge of this half platoon, 'Mate, remember, don't use that jug point . . . go up the hill a bit.' We settled down, I was staying round this little jungle base I'd set up on this day and they'd been gone for about 20 minutes, then boom, they got hit by a claymore mine. It knocked over the first three guys. He'd used the flat part.

We ran forward and I thought my heart was going to burst. We ran about a kilometre and a half through ankle-deep soft sand in our webbing and with our rifles and when we got there we found that the blokes who'd hit them with the mine had shot through very smartly. But we made an error and it was because we took the soft option.

The error and its consequences stayed with Cos.

That's why I think I stayed pretty what some would call zealous. I just had this thought that if you start cutting corners or half doing jobs, it can bring disaster. Imagine if late in the tour I'd been sent to check a place and it was a long way and it was a hot day so I just stopped halfway and radioed in that I'd checked it and it was clear, or looked around and thought, Oh the diggers are all very tired, we won't go there, and I just radioed in. What if that turned out to be something bad and somebody got affected by that? It comes down at the more macro sense to the fact that you've always got to be trustworthy, you must always do your job.

Diggers had their own way of describing a soldier who didn't pull his weight. He was called a 'Jack man', as in 'I'm all right, Jack' and it was someone who only worried about himself, not his mates. He was a despised character and a danger to everyone's safety. Cos learned that often the best way to protect others was to do your job correctly.

When I was a young platoon commander in the midst of battle I had to be tough as nails, prepared if necessary to walk past a wounded colleague, comrade, in order to prosecute the attack. The most I might do is say, 'You fix him,' but I had to be able to walk past that person.

When my three soldiers were wounded, my job when I got there was to first and foremost find out if the enemy was still there and what were we doing about it, if we didn't have that evidence. Was the place secure? And, thirdly, is somebody attending to the casualties.

Next, and most importantly, I had to call for the helicopters to come in and take them away. And that's before I could even say, 'Oh, it's Bill and Tom and Joe who've been hurt,' or how badly were they hurt?

I found out about how badly they were hurt in

calling for the helicopter because part of the questioning is how serious are these wounds? So you do have to get a grip on your own sense of compassion under certain circumstances, but that doesn't mean you should be absolute.

I think it's more appropriate to exhibit compassion as you get more senior in rank because your decisions will be quite far reaching, less instantaneous, so I should think that stifled compassion is more appropriate in the urgent and instantaneous needs of combat. But in any more measured activity you shouldn't be afraid of saying, Well, I'm going to do this but now I'll also start to measure how it can be done with a minimal human cost.

Cos' service in Vietnam was a turning point: in his career as a professional soldier; in his development as a leader; and as an individual. He spoke of it in an interview 35 years later with *The Army Newspaper*.

The discovery that I was suited to the lifestyle and that I enjoyed the confidence of my troops in combat meant a great deal to me, especially in that first crucial command where you wonder if you have what it takes.

EARLY
DAYS

2

★

**Tank Firing Range, Puckapunyal, Victoria,
28 July 1947**

Perched in the turret of his Matilda tank, Warrant
Officer John Cosgrove's practised eye picked up some
movement to his left rear. Years of training in the field
and his time in combat had given him a wide field of
acute vision. He briefly turned away from the ear-
splitting action in front of him and saw that the
movement was a jeep racing across the open fields
towards his position. He knew from the vehicle's speed
and direct route that it had to be carrying an important
message.

Turning back to his centre of attention he saw with
satisfaction that the gunners in the Matilda tanks he was
training were doing an excellent job in pulverising their

targets on the firing range. John Cosgrove had stayed on in the permanent army after the end of World War II and had been assigned to the newly formed School of Armour, based at Puckapunyal, about an hour's drive north of Melbourne. He brought with him the invaluable experiences of a combat veteran and he delighted in being able to pass on his hard-won wisdom to his charges. Today, he was in his element; in the field on the gunnery firing range putting the old Matilda tanks through their paces.

John Cosgrove signalled a ceasefire as the jeep pulled up in a cloud of dust. A keen young corporal jumped out, ran to his tank and handed up a telegram. Tearing it open, the veteran tried to ignore his thumping heart as he realised its significance. It was from his father-in-law, Bob Henrys, and it was short and so very sweet. It read: BORN WITH SPOUT STOP MOTHER AND CHILD BOTH WELL STOP CONGRATS BOB.

John and Ellen Cosgrove's second-born, Peter John Cosgrove, had entered the world. He arrived in Sydney's now-defunct Crown Street Women's Hospital, a brother for Stephanie, who was a fortnight away from her fourth birthday. As was the norm in those days, mum gave birth while dad went about his work. It didn't mean John Cosgrove wasn't overjoyed at the arrival of his son and heir; or that he wasn't filled with love and pride for his beloved Ellen. It was just the way things were done.

The beaming new dad immediately called an end to the gunnery practice and led his men and their machines back to the Sergeants' Mess, where he welcomed his boy over a few grogs before rushing off to organise leave to return to his family in Sydney.

John and Ellen Cosgrove were a devoted couple. They met early in the war, like countless other young Sydneysiders, while dancing at the famous old Trocadero nightspot in George Street. John Cosgrove was then a 25-year-old regular soldier. He'd enlisted in the Royal Australian Artillery in 1937 in Melbourne, where he was born and grew up. By the time he met Ellen he was a despatch rider for an artillery battery that was temporarily based at Ingleburn, in Sydney's west. Ellen Mary Henrys was a pretty 20-year-old working in the Army Pay Office at Victoria Barracks in Paddington. Their romance blossomed quickly and they married on Friday, 28 August 1942, a year after John had switched from the regular army to join the AIF.

Peter Cosgrove's father, John Cave Cosgrove, was largely a self-made man. Peter's grandfather, John Nereus Cosgrove, was a noted stage and film actor who died when his son John was nine. Peter's grandmother, Madeleine Treacey, struggled to raise John and his younger brother Bill on her modest wage as a librarian at the Central Catholic Library in Collins Street Melbourne.

When Madeleine died, aged 48, in 1933 in the depths of the Great Depression, John, then 17, and Bill, 14, were left to fend for themselves. They shared a flat in the working-class suburb of Richmond. John left school and, unable to find work, was forced to apply for government relief ('susso', subsistence payment for government-generated work). Bill continued at Christian Brothers

School at Eastern Hill for a while before he too left school and went on the dole. He would later recall the indignity of working for 'susso' on a road alongside the Yarra River, turning his face away in embarrassment when he saw a wealthy former schoolmate being driven past on his way to school.

As the economy picked up, John tried a variety of jobs – sales assistant for Kodak, plasterer's mate and tobacco salesman – before finding his niche in the regular army. It appealed to him because it offered the rare combination of food and accommodation, as well as regular income. John was at ease in uniform, and friends remember him always looking the part, cutting a fine figure on parade and often being chosen in honour guards. It was the start of a life-long dedication to the army.

★ ★ ★

Like many other young Australian couples during the war years, John and Ellen's marriage signified their optimism for a better future at a time when Australia was struggling through its darkest hours. On their wedding day young Australian diggers were locked in a desperate rear-guard guerrilla battle in the tiny hamlet of Isurava on the Kokoda Track in New Guinea trying to stave off a possible Japanese invasion.

Soon after the wedding, John's unit was posted to the Atherton Tableland in Queensland for training prior to embarkation to play out Australia's role in the Pacific War. Ellen followed John to Queensland while he trained, but when he was posted again they decided that she should return to Sydney where her mother was in frail health. John was determined his family would not suffer the same dislocations as he and his brother had. Wherever he was posted, Sydney would remain the family base.

Like countless other couples, John and Ellen endured long separations during the war. Ellen's loneliness and her anxiety at John's time on active service were eased by the birth of their first child, Stephanie, in August 1943. John served in the Pacific islands and in a variety of defence bases in Australia. At war's end, he remained in the permanent army – no doubt influenced, like so many of his generation, by the mental scars of his experiences during the Depression.

In the immediate post-war years, the army quickly shrank from almost half a million men down to a few thousand. John Cosgrove had risen to Warrant Officer but good postings were extremely scarce and he was forced to take whatever jobs were offered, even if they were far from Sydney. John would go to his posting and return home as often as he could while Ellen ran the family home in Sydney, while also caring for her mum and her dad, who was a World War I and World War II digger.

★ ★ ★

Ellen's father, Peter's maternal grandfather Bob Henrys, had been wounded several times in the critical battle to liberate the village of Villers-Bretonneux in France in World War I, where the Australians played a key role in saving the village. He was repatriated and, after regaining his health, he served in the permanent army between the wars. At the outbreak of World War II, he enlisted in the Second AIF and went away as the quartermaster sergeant of the 2/19th Battalion, part of the 8th Division, to Malaya. In the months before Pearl Harbor, Bob was struck down with a septic ulcer and was evacuated home. It was a lucky break. Then in his forties, and still somewhat frail from his World War I wounds, he would have been unlikely to survive the privations of Changi and the Burma Railway to which his comrades in the 8th Division were subjected following the fall of Singapore. Back home, Bob recovered from his ulcer and served out the rest of the war in base jobs in Australia.

★ ★ ★

Peter Cosgrove was clearly born into a khaki family. Many other members of his extended family served in the armed forces. Bob Henrys' brother, Ernie, fought in World War I and Ernie's sons served in World War II along with his daughter, Evaline, who joined the RAAF. Then there was Peter's uncle, Bill Cosgrove, who died as a Beaufighter pilot in New Guinea.

Toughened by the hardships of the Depression, Bill grew into a tall, strong young man who played three senior games for the Richmond Tigers Aussie Rules team before the war intervened. He inherited his father's baritone voice and love of the limelight and had an infectious zest for life. His dream had always been to fly. In June 1940, aged 21, he joined the RAAF, graduated as a pilot under the Empire Training Scheme and was posted to the Middle East. There, he saw service flying Blenheim light bombers in Abyssinia, Libya, Egypt and Iraq, before being transferred to Burma and Sumatra.

Bill was with 84 Squadron, operating out of North West Java when the Japanese closed in on Singapore in March 1942. Just as their aerodrome was about to be overrun by the rapidly advancing Japanese, Bill Cosgrove and 11 others escaped in a lifeboat and headed for Australia – a perilous journey of more than 2500 kilometres across the Indian Ocean. In one of the epic escapes of the war, the group, led by Wing Commander John Jeudwine of the RAF, survived an encounter with a Japanese submarine, a series of engine breakdowns, storms and sharks, and eventually made land near Shark Bay in Western Australia 44 days later.

After recovering from his ordeal, Bill Cosgrove was posted to 30 Squadron, flying Beaufighters in New Guinea in April 1943. He soon won renown for his audacious (some said reckless) flying and took part in many sorties there. By that time he was flying *Jack Dyer IV*. (Bill named all his planes after his football idol at his Richmond Tigers club, Jack Dyer, known to friend and foe as 'Captain Blood'. Bill flew the first *Jack Dyer* in Libya, the second in Sumatra and the third in Java.)

Ironically, *Jack Dyer IV* was being serviced and Bill was at the controls of a replacement plane when he crashed into the sea shortly after taking off from Goodenough Island on 11 August 1943. He was 24 years old. Bill left a widow, Dorothy, and a two-year-old daughter,

Madeleine. His beloved Tigers won the premiership later that year and their captain, Jack Dyer, dedicated the victory to Bill.

Bill's death hit his brother hard. John Cosgrove always spoke glowingly of Bill and young Peter Cosgrove grew up with a store of tales attesting to Bill's gallantry and sporting achievements

Another family story handed down, which Peter Cosgrove readily concedes may be apocryphal, holds that his father was part of a gun battery on Port Phillip Bay in Melbourne that claimed to have fired Australia's first angry shot of the war at a German merchant ship which headed out of the bay on the day war was declared. The shots missed their mark, perhaps luckily as it transpired that the ship's skipper was just trying to catch the tide. (This story sounds very similar to the oft-claimed 'first angry shot' of World War I where gunners from a battery at Port Phillip Bay were supposed to have fired warning shots at the German freighter *Pfalz* as it tried to flee hours after the declaration of war on 5 August 1914.)

★ ★ ★

Young Peter grew up in Underwood Street, in Paddington, Sydney, in a modest Victorian-era worker's terrace house with his parents, his sister, Stephanie, his grandfather, Bob Henrys, and his young cousin, Robert.

Paddo in the 1950s was a far cry from the elegant and exclusive suburb which today houses some of Sydney's social elite. The country was still emerging from the privations of the war. Life was male-dominated and unsophisticated. Families were bigger and houses were smaller. Children shared bedrooms with siblings, played street cricket and cowboys-and-Indians, made cubbies and billycarts, and dreamed of one day owning a Malvern Star bicycle. Few residents owned their own cars and the dunny carts still plied the back lanes to empty the neat rows of brick outhouses.

While Peter was in short pants, the Cosgroves lived opposite the Grand National Hotel – now a stylish London-style hotel and restaurant but in those days an unvarnished local watering hole where they hosed out the tiled floor of the public bar every evening after the six o'clock swill – the manic drinking rush forced on working men by the 6 pm closing laws. Peter learned a lot about human nature watching from his bedroom window facing the pub. He heard the raucous laughter of men in their cups, he witnessed fisticuffs and yelling matches and observed the local colourful characters.

Cos attended pre-school at Peter Pan Kindergarten in Paddington. It was here that his sister Stephanie first observed the stirrings of his leadership skills when, as a three-and-a-half-year-old, he led a revolt to escape over the wall. The coup d'état arose over dissatisfaction with the fish in white sauce being served for lunch. It was a harbinger of two Cosgrove traits that would emerge in Peter in subsequent years: a propensity for direct action and an enduring fondness for food.

Family members recall Peter as a bright but often headstrong boy with abundant reserves of energy who idolised his dad and treasured his time at his side when

John was not on duty. John Cosgrove was regularly away on his various postings and, as has long been the way in army families, it was often left to Ellen to draw the discipline boundaries for her restless young son. Peter would occasionally leave home when he didn't get his own way. Ellen knew the 'runaway' routine and would keep the young tearaway in sight as he headed off down the road. For his part, Peter would look back to make sure Ellen was watching.

Peter went off to big school at five, joining big sister Stephanie at St Francis of Assisi Primary School, less that half a kilometre away on the other side of Oxford Street, almost in the shadows of Victoria Barracks, where his dad would occasionally be stationed.

Primary school was a largely carefree time of chasings, hidings and Cocky Laura in the schoolyard, of warm milk at morning playtime and Vegemite sandwiches in brown paper bags for lunch, of learning times-tables by rote and finding out that the pink bits on the map were our empire, of desks with inkwells and dip-in pens with rose nibs, of minor skirmishes between the Catholics and the 'publics' on the way home, of hours of street cricket, toy soldiers and the occasional bombardment with chokos from the vines on the back fence.

Peter wore his best clothes to Sunday Mass and proceeded through his First Confession, First Communion and on to his Confirmation. At the same time he balanced things with a constant diet of books. The Harry Potters of the time for boys were *The Adventures of Biggles*,

Treasure Island and *Robinson Crusoe*. Like most kids of his generation, Peter's imagination was fired up by sitting around the family bakelite radio and listening to serials like *Superman*, *Tarzan*, *Hop Harrigan* and *The Search for the Golden Boomerang*.

It was a simpler world: before corner shops and local grocers were swamped by supermarkets; before designer labels; where milkos still delivered each morning; when almost every man and woman wore a hat; where people re-soled their shoes and wore them to within an inch of their lives; when dinner was almost always meat and three veg and dogs and cats got the leftovers; where polio and diphtheria threatened; and eating out meant going to the local Chinese restaurant once in a blue moon.

During his formative years the two most influential men in Peter's life had a lasting impact on him. Peter spent hours at his grandad Bob Henrys' knee. He sat with him, and his dad, and listened to the mesmerising ABC radio coverage of test cricket matches, stimulating a life-long love of cricket and most other sports. He listened to Bob's fascinating tales of fighting with the Anzacs in faraway lands. He felt the shrapnel bumps on the old soldier's cheek, wounds received at Villers-Bretonneux 30 years earlier. As Peter got older, Bob gradually opened up to him and allowed him to draw out the stories of his years as a soldier. Peter would later admit to hero-worshipping Bob Henrys and credited him, along with his father, as being a major influence in his choice of career.

Despite his unavoidable absences on duty, John

Cosgrove was a devoted father who provided a fine role model for Peter, as he acknowledged many years later.

> He taught me that you've got to be absolutely reliable. My dad was. I knew that from what I saw as a young fella and then confirmed it when I was in my very early years in the army – that he was rock-solid. His word was his bond. John Cosgrove was reliable. If he said he would do something then everybody knew that he would move heaven and earth to do it. So his mates, his superiors, his subordinates could rely on him. So it was this notion that at the core of a soldier is somebody who must and can be trusted.

As he matured, Peter also developed a deep and loving connection with his mother. Ellen Cosgrove was, in many ways, a woman ahead of her time. She loved listening to the radio coverage of Federal Parliament and she read extensively about contemporary politics and economic affairs. She held strong views on these and other subjects and wasn't afraid to air them. She took a keen interest in her children's progress at school and encouraged them to chase their goals.

The Cosgroves had moved to an army flat in Belgrave Street, Bronte, in Sydney's eastern suburbs, by the time Peter grew into long pants. He began his secondary schooling a few streets away at Waverley College, a Catholic boys' high school run by the Christian Brothers.

Bronte was redolent of middle-class Sydney during

the 1960s. It was an established beachside suburb, a sprawl of red-tiled roofs blanketing the high ground from Birrell Street down to the grassy gully leading to Bronte's popular surf beach. It was a vast improvement on Paddington for a sports-mad boy, with an array of parks, ovals and reserves all within easy walking distance.

Peter's new school was in the middle of a sustained growth spurt, with more than 1000 pupils. Waverley was a member of the Combined Associated Schools, along with St Aloysius' College, Barker College, Cranbrook School, Knox Grammar and Trinity Grammar. By the time Peter went there, Waverley was almost 60 years old and had built a reputation for its sporting prowess.

The Christian Brothers were noted for their vigorous approaches to discipline and sport. Along with most of their contemporaries, the brothers wielded leather straps with enthusiasm. Peter copped at least his fair share. The brothers also sought, and usually achieved, success on the sporting field and had produced a crop of outstanding sportsmen. Peter Cosgrove wasn't one of them. Although he was a passionate sports lover, Peter is remembered as a wholehearted trier, rather than a star. He played in the lower grades at rugby and cricket. He was not built for speed and his strength had not yet developed.

Peter stood out in three areas at Waverley: English, for which he had a natural bent; independent thought, which brought him considerable strife on occasion; and a flair for leadership in the school's cadet corps.

The new medium of television was fast expanding into houses in Australian capitals and Peter's world expanded as he was exposed to the best of contemporary American culture by watching shows like *77 Sunset Strip, Jet Jackson, Perry Mason, Adventures in Paradise* and *The Three Stooges.* Australian TV contributed *Bandstand, Six O'Clock Rock, Bob Dyer's Pick a Box* and *Four Corners.*

As with many private schools at the time, it was compulsory to join the cadet unit at Waverley College. The experience had a differing impact on different characters. Two of Peter's contemporaries in his cadet unit would later go to gaol for their refusal to accept National Service during the Vietnam War. Peter felt a natural affiliation for the cadet unit and he showed early promise. Each year Waverley would send one member of its cadet unit who showed signs of outstanding potential on a visit to the Royal Military College, Duntroon, in Canberra. Peter won the honour in his second year in the cadets. Aged 14, he spent four days immersed in the intoxicating atmosphere of the institution that was charged with producing Australia's elite military officers. Many years later, Peter would call it 'a place of grim purpose and hard edges' but also 'a place of rich beauty and history, of timeless military liturgy, of humanity and warmth'. During his visit Peter stayed in the same accommodation as the Duntroon staff cadets. He ate with them, saw them on parade, at sport and in action, and witnessed the full range of weapons and armoured vehicles they used on manoeuvres. He even attended some lectures. It was a heady experience. Peter had always thought he might follow his father into the army. Now he was resolved to make the army his career.

Back at Waverley, Peter focused on cadets with a new diligence. He won respect from both his superiors and his peers for his conscientious efforts as he progressed through the ranks. Nevertheless, schoolmates recall that he was still able to be one of the boys even as he exercised his leadership skills. It would be a trait often commented on throughout his army career.

His efforts in the cadets didn't prevent Peter from expressing his considerable independence in other areas of school life. He was a gifted writer but didn't always use his powers for good. He copped a lot of flak for his involvement in an unauthorised magazine, which did the rounds at the school. It was just a handful of loose pages that included some satirical spoofs on some of the prominent Brothers – a naughty schoolboy send-up. It led to a witch-hunt just before his Leaving Certificate exams. Peter was an early suspect because of his well-recognised language skills but he weathered the storm. It was just as well because he had decided to repeat his final year after disappointing results. He would later admit to cruising academically in his first attempt at the Leaving Certificate, the equivalent of today's Higher School Certificate. He described himself at the time as 'smart but lazy'.

The first time round I was pretty young for the Leaving. I did it at 16 and then I discovered I could sneak into pubs, I discovered going out with my mates on Friday evening, I didn't work very hard and got a rotten pass in the first year but

I'd almost given up, knowing that I'd probably repeat anyway.

In fact, more than half of Peter's class repeated their final year. The extra year of maturity gave many of them a different attitude towards their teachers. They had lost their awe of them and some (and Peter was often among them) discovered a new-found confidence that bordered on cheekiness. Classmates remember Peter as something of a stirrer that year. He often bucked authority and revealed a determination and single-mindedness in standing up for his views and for himself. He'd developed into an excellent raconteur, perhaps channelling some of his grandfather Jack Cosgrove's thespian skills in capturing and holding an audience and in his fine comic touch.

In his final year Peter was appointed Waverley's senior cadet underofficer. Every Friday afternoon, he would take command of the unit's parade and march his cadets from Henrietta Street down to Waverley Oval where they would train under their platoon commanders. He would oversee their training and then he would march them back to the old tennis courts. There, he'd address them with the same confidence he would display to the Australian public decades later.

When the 1964 Leaving Certificate loomed, Peter knuckled down and put in some late hard yards of study. His efforts paid off and he headed to Canberra, armed with a solid Leaving Certificate pass and high hopes.

THE FLYING COSGROVES 3

Peter Cosgrove's military heritage extended back further than his grandfather, beginning with his great-great-grandfather, Thomas Cosgrove, who was a private in the British Army.

Born in Killskerry parish in County Tyrone in Northern Ireland on 28 March 1806, Thomas enlisted in the 89th Regiment of Foot at Enniskillen on 24 May 1822. He served in the regiment for almost seven years and saw action in Burma in 1824, where he was shot in his left arm. He recovered to serve in Rangoon in lower Burma and Poonamallee, a garrison town near Madras in India, and returned to Ireland before being invalided out of the army in 1830, aged 24. The following year,

Thomas married Mary Blakely in Dromore, a poor farming area in County Tyrone. They had four children before the lure of a new life in the colony of Sydney saw them leave Ireland in 1841, a few years ahead of the calamitous potato famine. Even before the blight hit the vital potato crop in 1845, Ireland was a desperately poor country as the noted French sociologist, Gustave de Beaumont, noted when he visited in 1835.

> I have seen the Indian in his forests, and the Negro in his chains, and thought, as I contemplated their pitiable condition, that I saw the very extreme of human wretchedness; but I did not know the condition of unfortunate Ireland. In all countries, more or less, paupers may be discovered; but an entire nation of paupers is what was never seen until it was shown in Ireland.

It was little wonder that Thomas and Mary Cosgrove jumped at the chance of a new life in Sydney. The family sailed on 10 April 1841 on the *Herald* – one of many ships taking Irish emigrants to England, the United States, Canada and Australia. These transports became known as 'coffin ships' because of the huge attrition rate suffered en route by the weakened travellers.

Sadly, the Cosgroves added to those losses when their youngest boy, Patrick, died during the voyage. After 99 days at sea the *Herald* reached Sydney on 15 July 1841. Thomas and Mary and their surviving sons, John, Joseph and Thomas Junior, began their new life in Wollongong, about 80 kilometres south of Sydney, where Thomas had been promised work as a labourer on the Osborne Estate, owned by a prominent Irish settler.

The family flourished down under. Thomas and Mary had four more children – William, Nancy, Samuel and Mary Jane – and Thomas was eventually able to buy 57 acres in what is now known as Mt Keira, on the outskirts of Wollongong. There, helped by his children, he worked the farm, growing produce for the Sydney markets and breeding horses. Thomas died in 1864, from 'inflammation of the liver' – often code in those days for a heavy drinker. His widow Mary lived to 98.

Peter's great-grandfather, Thomas Cosgrove Junior, was 22 when he married Ellen Condon at Shellharbour in 1857. Ellen was the daughter of James Condon, who had been sent to Sydney as a convict in 1822, and Mary Condon, who emigrated from County Cork as a free settler in 1832. James had been convicted of breaking a curfew imposed under the Irish Insurrection Acts, aimed at controlling Catholic rebels intent on overturning the existing religious laws, which effectively prevented Catholics from voting.

By the time Thomas Junior and Ellen married, their respective families were well established in the Wollongong area. They followed the family tradition and produced 11 children over almost 20 years. Thomas farmed and bred horses so successfully that he eventually bought the Steam Packet Hotel in Shellharbour. He later sold it and moved, first to the Sutton Forest area and then to Moss Vale, where he became known as a prosperous, if occasionally obstreperous, store owner, publican and local identity.

Around 1879, Thomas and Ellen left their rural life and headed for the big smoke of Sydney. Thomas bought a sizable chunk of property in Castlereagh Street. It ran from Market Street to Park Street and extended through to Elizabeth Street. He took over the licence of the Bushman's Club Hotel in Castlereagh Street (near the site of the present City Tattersall's Club), changed its name to the Turf Club and renovated it. He also became an auctioneer and built stables and a horse market that faced Elizabeth Street.

Thomas timed his move to Sydney beautifully. He arrived just as the city entered a land boom and the population was in a massive growth spurt. Sydney's population grew from 135,000 in 1871 to 462,000 by the turn of the century, buoyed by the gold rushes and developments like the telegraph, the multi-gauge railway linking the capital cities from Brisbane to Adelaide and the steam tram.

As the Cosgroves settled into their new home, Sydney was rapidly transforming into a substantial metropolis. The first woodblocks were being laid in King Street, the start of the gradual replacement of the city's macadamised roads, the elegant Strand Arcade was being constructed after the fashion of London's Burlington Arcade, and the steam tram was running from the central terminus at Redfern down to the Botanic Gardens.

The southern end of Elizabeth Street, where the Cosgroves lived, was Sydney's equine centre. It had grown up around Hyde Park, the site of the city's first racecourse. Although the racing action had by then moved to Randwick, the area was still home to sale yards, stables and saddlers. The Cosgrove kids were plucked from their tranquil rural lifestyle and suddenly thrust into the hustle of bookmakers, punters, jockeys and the usual attendant 'colourful racing identities'.

Thomas and Ellen Cosgrove's seventh child was John Nereus Cosgrove, Peter's grandfather, born on 18 May 1867. Known as Jack, he was named after an early Christian martyr, Saint Nereus, whose feast day fell on his birthday. (Coincidentally, this was yet another indirect Cosgrove military connection as Saint Nereus was a Roman soldier who converted to Christianity and then refused to serve any longer as a soldier. Not surprisingly, perhaps, he was put to death for his beliefs.)

Jack Cosgrove would provide the second major strain in Peter's bloodline – the lure of the limelight. Thomas hoped that Jack would follow his saintly namesake and join the priesthood but was proved well off the mark. Jack became a noted stage and film actor and later a theatrical manager. With two of his brothers, Will and Tom, Jack Cosgrove went on to form 'The Flying Cosgroves', a touring vaudeville-style performance group.

Jack and his brother William were initially sent to St Mary's School, part of the magnificent St Mary's Cathedral complex, an easy walk across Hyde Park from their home. It was a tough transition from their earlier rustic education, as Jack would later write:

We were funny little bumpkins, with our hair cut long, country fashion, and we were dressed in pinafores. The other fellows used to call us Mary Anne and Bridget, and brother Will would let go of my hand, which he always held, to deal out stoush to the scoffing townies. It took us both some time, and cost us a few 'blood noses' to convince the school that they must treat us with respect.

In 1881, in pursuit of their hope that Jack would gravitate towards the priesthood, Thomas and Ellen enrolled him at St Joseph's College, then in Harrington Street in The Rocks (behind the present-day St Patrick's Church). Later that year, the school's boarders moved to its current location at Hunter's Hill, where the school would develop into one of Sydney's leading Greater Public Schools. Jack left shortly after the move. He turned to the theatre, starting in the vaudeville productions at the Tivoli.

Growing up in Sydney city during the 1880s, Jack and his siblings immersed themselves in the vibrant city's core activities: horseracing and the theatre. Just north of their home, around King Street, Sydney's theatrical district was buzzing in answer to the city's demand for entertainment. In 1879, one of the great figures in Australian theatrical history, James Cassius (J.C.) Williamson produced and starred in the Gilbert and Sullivan comic opera *HMS Pinafore* at the Theatre Royal in King Street. It was a roaring success and led to a series of Gilbert and Sullivan productions, spawning a burgeoning industry. The Victoria Theatre flourished in Pitt Street near the Strand Arcade and Her Majesty's opened in 1887 on the corner of Pitt and Market streets. Sydney's theatre-going audiences had reached sufficient sophistication by 1891 that J.C. Williamson was able to persuade the finest actress of the age, the 'Divine' Sarah Bernhardt, to perform *Camille* at Her Majesty's.

The Cosgroves were enthusiastic theatre-goers and the kids were exposed to the glamour and the excitement from an early age. Jack and Will were captivated. But their plans for a career on the stage were postponed when Thomas found himself in financial difficulties. Thomas was widely regarded as a fine judge of horseflesh but he was also noted for an unpredictable, and sometimes violent, temper that saw him sail close to the wind with the authorities. This, combined with the inevitable decline in the horse trade and the onset of the 1890 depression, saw him fall into debt and head off to try his luck in the Western Australian goldfields in 1891.

Thomas used his auctioneering and wheeler-dealer skills to set up in business in Coolgardie, 550 kilometres north-east of Perth, where the biggest gold rush in Australian history was in full swing. While a seemingly endless stream of thousands of hopeful prospectors chased their dreams in the goldfields, Thomas and his brother William profited by providing them with access to ready cash by auctioning their horses, tools and equipment. Over the next few years Coolgardie's population swelled to 15,000, making it the third largest town in

Western Australia, with more than 700 mining companies from there floated in London. By 1898 the town boasted two stock exchanges, seven newspapers and 23 hotels.

Thomas lived the big life. Jack later spent a couple of years living with him in Coolgardie but came back east to join his mother and the rest of the family. Thomas never returned to his wife and family. He died of a heart attack in the goldfields, aged 67, in 1902.

In Sydney, Jack briefly tried his hand at a few menial jobs before joining Alfred Dampier's Theatre Company, delivering his first line in the company's production of *Othello*. A string of extra work followed before he won a part as a juvenile lead in a company that toured New Zealand and then the Victorian goldfields. By 1888, Jack was playing leading roles at the major theatres in Sydney and Melbourne. He won wide acclaim as a comedy actor in a series of Victorian melodramas and secured a contract with the Bland Holt Company that stretched out to eight years. During this time, he showed that he had a prodigious memory as well as a penchant for practical jokes. While he was with Bland Holt, Jack became one of the best-known performers in the country. Unlike many actors, he found fame and success early and he enjoyed the good times without reserve. He would later lament that his success came too quickly and it went to his head.

Always a solid drinker, Jack began to let this trait affect his professional and personal life. He was honest in his self-appraisal and later conceded, 'I became fat and lost my ambition.' By the end of their association, Jack happily admitted that Holt treated him better than he deserved. Jack decided to strike out on his own and launched a career as a theatrical producer – sadly, with little success.

Jack regularly joined forces with his older brother Will and youngest brother Tom and they toured throughout rural and regional Australia as 'The Flying Cosgroves'. The name was apparently a spoof on a popular act touring Australia at the time, The Flying Jordans, a family of genuine trapeze artists from San Francisco. The Cosgrove boys, especially Jack, were clearly not built for aerial heroics and they used the gag to great effect as they travelled the countryside. They formed a versatile troupe and each variously handled the many roles, on and off stage, required of a small travelling theatrical company. Nevertheless, it was little more than subsistence living and on many occasions people claimed 'The Flying Cosgroves' name referred to their ability to get out of town before their creditors got to them.

Will was the steadiest character of the trio and had considerable individual success as a producer. He created the Cosgrove Musical Comedy Company and often wrote its productions, usually comic melodramas. Many were adapted from the London stage but he also rode on the groundswell of developing Australian national pride by writing a number of popular plays with local themes. The three brothers often interchanged roles and won considerable popular, if not critical, acclaim. A steady stream of successful productions brought Will financial security but Jack's bohemian lifestyle saw him fritter away his earnings. Jack's occasional forays into management were also unsuccessful, and despite a growing celebrity he was usually battling to find money. He was widely regarded as talented but lazy and his indolence apparently eventually caused a rift between him and Will.

Jack was also a bit of a lad with the ladies. He married twice, first in Melbourne to Florence Emily Belcher in 1893. Their first child, a daughter, was born prematurely and died in December 1894. Their second daughter was born just after Christmas (and therefore named Noël) the following year in New Zealand, where Jack was performing.

Florence acted under the name of Flo Dillon and joined Jack on the stage in a number of productions. Later young Noël sometimes also played children's roles. Sadly, Florence contracted meningitis while they were running a theatre in Adelaide and died, aged just 27, in January 1902. The following year, Jack took up with English-born actress Mildred Nunnerley. Their daughter, Angela Madeline, was born on 1 June 1903 and they married on 29 July. Over the next few years Jack's work flourished but his home life floundered as his drinking and carousing increased. Mildred left him and they were eventually divorced in 1913.

Jack's star had fallen substantially by now and he was constantly trying to cadge money from relatives, friends and acquaintances, earning himself (or perhaps bestowing on himself) the nickname 'The Great Australian Bite'. He turned his misfortune and his reputation into a rich vein of material for his comic turns, both on and off the stage. But worse was to come for Jack when, in November 1915, his daughter Noël succumbed after a long battle with tuberculosis, just before her twentieth birthday. While Jack was nursing Noël he met Madeleine Stephanie Treacey. They would never marry because Madeleine had been divorced once and was still married to another, but they would have three children together: Stephanie, who died in infancy; Peter Cosgrove's father, John Cave Francis Cosgrove, born on 11 January 1916; and Peter's uncle, William Nicholas Pax Cosgrove, born on Armistice Day (11 November) 1918 (*pax* is Latin for peace).

★ ★ ★

In addition to his varied stage career, Jack Cosgrove was one of the pioneers of the Australian film industry. The family historian, Jenny Rudd O'Neill, believes he may have had a role in *The Story of the Kelly Gang*, made in 1906 and recognised as the world's first feature movie. It's difficult to confirm or disprove as only a few scenes survive but Jack is supposed to have told family members that he played a policeman in a Ned Kelly movie. Perhaps he was in another movie on the subject made around 1920. What is certain is that Jack did star in a number of silent movies during a golden period in cinema in Australia through the 1920s. His credits included such memorable titles as *The Luck of the Roaring Camp*, *Driving a Girl to Distraction*, *While the Billy Boils*, *The Gentleman Bushranger* and *Possum Paddock*. By this stage Jack was not only growing in renown but also relentlessly growing in size. (On one photo taken at a Perth race meeting in 1923, one of his friends has written 'Fat but fit' over Jack's massive frame. It shows Jack wearing a straw boater, looking the spitting image of W.C. Fields, with his coat fighting a losing battle to contain his bulging girth.)

Around this time Jack tried producing and writing his own films, as well as starring in them. Two survived: *Silks and Saddles* and *Sunshine Sally*. Jack wrote them both and in each he pokes fun at his size.

Jack's size and prodigious appetite began to take its toll and by the end of 1922, his health began to fail. He continued to work, probably trying to build up a nest egg for Madeleine and their two boys, but by 1925 he was in and out of Sydney Hospital. He died on 11 August 1925. *The Bulletin* of 20 August 1925 said:

> John Cosgrove, hero of a hundred racy yarns, will spin them no more. His stout and cheerful presence was familiar to theatregoers from Kalgoorlie to Cooktown, and in the profession he was esteemed for the best part of 40 years as a prince of greenroom jesters, and a very good actor withal.

There's little doubt that Jack Cosgrove's thespian genes found their way through to his grandson, as any observer of Peter Cosgrove performing on parade, on a stage or in the limelight will readily attest.

CADET COSGROVE 4

COSGROVE PJ

In January 1965, 17-year-old Peter Cosgrove stepped off the train at Canberra's Kingston Station and joined a group of bright-eyed young men lugging their bags to the bus that would take them the last few kilometres to the start of their new life at the Royal Military College at Duntroon.

Peter had been waiting for this day for years and he was gripped by a bubbling anticipation, tempered by the nervous desire to make a good impression with both his fellow cadets and his instructors. Above all, though, he was buoyed by a firm belief that he was up to the challenge. After all, he was one of around 50 successful applicants, out of more than 250, who applied for a Duntroon scholarship in 1964 and who, along with another 50 or so normal-entry cadets, made up the 109 hopefuls of 1965 – the biggest intake yet seen by the college.

His early confidence was put to the test as soon as he took his seat on the bus.

I found myself sitting next to a very impressive-looking young man, a fellow new cadet. We introduced ourselves, Peter Cosgrove. Grant Chaseling. I thought I'd strike up a conversation so I asked him where he went to school and he said, King's, one of Sydney's very prestigious public schools.

I said, 'Oh, and were you active in school affairs, were you a prefect?'

And he said, 'Oh, yes, I was the captain of the school.'

I said, 'Oh, very good. What about football, did you play rugby?'

'Yes, I was captain of the 1st Fifteen and captain of the GPS 1sts.' I said, 'Were you in the cadets?'

He said, 'Yeah, I was the senior cadet.'

I said, 'What about cricket?'

He said, 'Oh, I didn't play cricket. I didn't have time – I was the stroke of the rowing eight.'

Then, he turned to me and said, 'What about you?'

I said, 'I'm on the wrong bus, mate!'

Cos' confidence would have been even further dented had he known back then what he found out many years later when he was permitted to look at his files.

> I know now that I squeaked into Duntroon. I'm well aware that the board wasn't wholly persuaded of my field marshal-type qualities at the time they considered my application because the casting vote of the Chairman was necessary to get me onto the successful candidates list.

That prescient selection committee chairman must have seen some potential in the candidate who stood before him that even Cos found difficult to discern on reflection.

> When I look back at it I was still pretty immature. Notwithstanding the fact that I loved what I knew of the army through my dad's service, it didn't make me necessarily an organised, self-disciplined, highly self-confident individual. These are things you have to inculcate and grow. I don't think I shone through on the interview board as being, 'Oh, we must have this guy.'

Cos had no time to stew on any doubts. From the moment a cadet enters Duntroon until he finally throws his hat into the air at the end of his graduation parade, he is stretched to his physical, emotional and psychological extremities. Cos' class was paraded on arrival on the famous Duntroon 'Square', where they were confronted by the college's stentorian Regimental Sergeant Major (RSM), Tom Muggleton, and a posse of 'drillies' (or drill sergeants). Then they were driven along like harried cattle with a cacophony of ear-splitting commands as they were subjected to the introductory routine for the new batch of Fourth Class Cadets. Fourth Class was Duntroon's lowest of the low – no responsibilities and no privileges.

The new boys of 1965 hit the ground running. They had to march everywhere at the double and swing their arms with an exaggerated parade-ground action. They were reduced to a surname, albeit usually prefixed by 'Mister'. 'Mister Cosgrove, get here at the double!' Fourth Class polished the floors, cleaned the toilets, the urinals, the baths and the sinks. And they were at the beck and call of their seniors.

They had to immediately conform to time-honoured Duntroon routines. Each cadet had his own room, where every item of clothing had to be placed on the shelves in neat piles measuring 9 inches high and 9 inches wide, shirts, singlets, underpants, socks to be wound up a certain way and put in the drawers. Shoes and boots had to be gleaming, laced correctly and lined up across the bottom of the cupboard in the correct order, finishing with sandshoes. Every room had to be laid out in identical fashion so instructors or seniors could open the door and see two hats, shirts, singlets, underpants, socks, etcetera – all in perfect lines – and uniforms, greatcoat and webbing hung in the correct positions. Thursdays were special inspection days as beds had to be made up immaculately with geometrically square corners. On their beds, on a piece of calico cloth, each cadet laid out his rifle, dismantled with bayonet, scabbard, magazines, gas plug, spring and ancillary parts all lined up in the prescribed order.

Three of Cos' new classmates bailed out in the first week. They left even before the class faced its first major challenge – the three-week bush orientation camp at Point Hut on the Murrumbidgee River, about 40 kilometres south of Canberra. Cos had been on cadet camps before but this was a quantum leap outside his comfort zone. He came armed with his theoretical cadet-unit knowledge. He knew how to pull apart a Bren gun: 'pistol, barrel, butt, body, bipod . . .' He knew how to march, fire a weapon and read a map. But, sweltering in a 40-degree Canberra summer wearing a World War II American-style tin helmet, showering in the open, shaving without soap in cold water, battling over obstacle courses and doing physical training in a roughly shaved paddock, lying on bristly cornstalks, Cos realised he was less physically prepared than he'd thought. He struggled to keep pace with some of his classmates, especially those who were emerging as the group's outstanding athletes, like Grant Chaseling, the bloke he'd met on the bus. Being fair of complexion also added to his discomfort and he battled on with cracked lips and blisters from sunburn. Through these early trials, Cos kept his spirits high and maintained his infectious sense of humour. He struck up what would become a life-long friendship with one of his classmates, Mike McDermott. Mike was an outstanding schoolboy athlete and was having an easier time than Cos.

> I remember admiring how Cos battled on, even though it was clear he was having problems with some things. I found I had no physical problems. When I went there I was fit, a high school runner and footballer. Plus I'd worked in some factories and I had a bit more upper-body strength than some of the others. I could do chin-ups and climb ropes and they were the things Cos had problems with. I remember one time he had to climb up a rope and then go across it and then down. He just couldn't do it. He had to go back on Friday afternoons and do it. But he eventually did it!

Both Cos and Mike were assigned to Kokoda Company, one of the four companies making up the Royal Military College Corps of Staff Cadets – Alamein, Gallipoli, Kapyong and Kokoda (all named after iconic battles). Kokoda had the reputation for the toughest discipline in Duntroon's hyper-competitive world and life quickly turned into a constant slog for Cos. His early fitness difficulties doomed him to extended periods of extra drills. He found himself trapped in a cycle; the more extra drills he copped, the more likely he was to attract another drill because of the added pressure. He would get up at a quarter past five, to get ready for the extra drill at six o'clock for an hour. Then he would race back to clean his room before rushing back for the regular parade. But the instructors would usually find something – dust in the welts of his shoes, a smudge of Brasso on his badge, a twisted bootlace, or a speck of dust down his barrel – so he would end up with another extra drill parade, prolonging the cycle. He also attracted his share of the other punishments on offer: CB (confinement to barracks); and SOL (stoppage of leave).

One regular form of hazing (the accepted term for harassment or bastardisation) faced by Fourth Class would come when a senior class man arrived and announced, 'You're all on parade. I want you back here in 2 minutes, in PT gear. Go!' The unfortunates would run back a kilometre to their blocks in their boots and webbing, rifle and helmet, strip, change into PT gear and run back, to be greeted with, 'Right, I want you back here in blue ceremonial, go!' These torments were called leaps. The aim was to teach you how to handle pressure, to manage time, to be organised and have yourself ready to withstand the onslaught.

One of Cos' classmates, Harvey Shore, who became a successful television producer, wrote of the 1965 system:

> Fourth Class were the lowest of the low (in cadet-speak, Fourth Class were the 'shit of shits'). Third Class were still junior classmen in the hierarchy, but a step up the ladder and therefore known as the 'shit of kings'. Second Class were senior cadets with some little power and with responsibility for bastardisation. They were sometimes the terror of

Fourth Class, and therefore known as the 'king of shits'. The top of the ladder was First Class, the most senior year. Its members were known as 'king of kings' . . . they looked after the junior cadets too, but were generally totally absorbed in completing their final year at Royal Military College (RMC) and graduating into the regular army.

Hazing reached a peak during Cos' time at Duntroon. Some activities seemed to have some benefits. For example, Fourth Class cadets had to memorise the ABC Morning News before they arrived at breakfast. They couldn't eat until the senior cadets were all seated and they had successfully taken turns to recite the various news items. This could be said to promote an awareness of current affairs and improve memory and presentation – even if it also meant those who tripped up missed out on their meal. The same couldn't be said for practices like 'square meals', where a cadet would have to laboriously eat his food sitting rigidly upright and moving his hands in straight lines, up vertically from his plate in line with his mouth and then horizontally to his mouth and back, with every single mouthful. Nor did there seem to be merit in standing under a freezing shower while whistling 'God Save the Queen', or 'Wet Twos', where a cadet was forced to stand clothed under a shower until two minutes before the evening meal. Then he had to undress, dry himself, dress in his formal uniform and race the 100 metres to the mess. If he was late he would cop an extra drill and often the punishment cycle would continue.

Mind you, Cos and Mike McDermott brought some of the torment on themselves. They both maintained a healthy disrespect for pomposity and enjoyed matching their wits with the seniors with exchanges like: 'What are you two up to? Why aren't you on parade?' 'Look, could you do us a favour and tell the RSM that we can't make the parade today but we'll definitely come tomorrow . . . both of us . . . and we'll be early!'

One night they were wandering back to their barracks very late after a few beers when they realised that someone was walking some distance behind them. They ducked into the shadows and saw a man with outstanding bearing, resplendent in his uniform, boots gleaming in the moonlight. To their horror they instantly recognised the figure as the most feared man in the college, the RSM. They felt confident that he hadn't spotted them and, after all, it was three in the morning and the RSM was actually coming home later than them. But the next day on parade on a baking hot summer day on 'The Square', as the beads of alcoholic sweat gathered on their brows, they could feel the RSM's eyes boring into them. That in itself was a wonder because in the glaring sun his eyes were tiny slits the width of a cigarette paper. His thrice-shaved face glistened with a red tinge as he roared, 'Cosgrove . . . twisted bootlace. One extra drill!'

Both Cos and Mike strained to surreptitiously look down at the offending boots. Sure enough, the RSM was right. The bloody RSM was always right . . . even when he wasn't!

★ ★ ★

The pressure on the new cadets even continued during meals. On command from their seniors, Fourth Class had to recite a litany of traditional Duntroon useless pieces of knowledge, known as 'the screed test'. For example, they had to commit to memory the inscription on the grave of Major General Sir William Bridges, Duntroon's founding commandant.

> Major General Sir William Throsby Bridges, KCB, CMG, died 18 May 1915 from wounds received on Gallipoli Peninsula whilst in command of the Australian Imperial Force. A gallant and erudite soldier, he was the first Commandant of this College, where in recognition of faithful service, his remains were publicly interred on 3 September 1915.

Cadets learned that Bridges was the only soldier, of more than 60,000 who died overseas in World War I, whose remains were returned home for burial. His horse, Sandy, was the only one of 160,000 sent overseas during that war to be brought back.

They also had to know descriptions of each of the peculiar Seven Wonders of Duntroon: the bell that never tolls (a relic of the original meeting place on the edge of 'The Square'); the backward boomerangs (an error in the

Corps of Staff Cadets' badge in front of their Mess); General Graves' Bridge (a play on General Bridges' Grave that referred to an old bridge on the firing range); the 'room within a room' (a secretly hideaway built in the late 1950s by a cadet under the floor of his room); the steps that lead to nowhere (old steps near the Cork and Beer Blocks); the mast without a ship (the flagpole); and the Kokoda Trail (the path leading to General Bridges' grave). They had to learn other oddities, like 'How high is the flagpole?' 'The height of the flagpole is seventy-five feet, six and a half inches, allowing for atmospheric vari-ation and bird droppings, Sir!' They found that chairs were 'for Fourth Class to sit six inches from and parallel to, Third Class to sit on, Second Class to lounge on and to stop First Class from falling on to the floor.' Any time a cadet failed to recite the requested piece word-perfectly, he would be hit with punishments ranging from push-ups to extra drills, or perhaps some other specially concocted 'torture'.

★ ★ ★

While most of the hazing was akin to the normal 'ragging' that went on in many boarding schools and universities at the time, some bastardisation became more personal, and occasionally it left physical or psychologi-cal scars. Fortunately, for most of Fourth Class it only lasted for the first three to six months of their first year. It usually began to ease after the annual Lanyard Parade, which signified the completion of their initial training, and meant they were entitled to wear the khaki lanyard of the Corps of Staff Cadets. The system was generally accepted by the authorities, who regarded it as part of the toughening process necessary to produce officers capable of command.

But things were changing at Duntroon. Cos' class was the second intake since the college had linked with the University of New South Wales to provide its graduates with a university degree. The initiative created considerable animosity from the current senior classes who realised they would not receive a degree. Some felt their successors would have a career advantage as university graduates. It also led to sharp philosophical differences between the college's academic staff and its military staff. The academics saw many of the traditional hazing activities as unnecessary impediments to the cadets' studies. The military staff saw them as essential rites of passage. The end result was an upsurge in bastardisation.

It came to a head in 1969, the year after Cos graduated, when a college lecturer, Gerald Walsh, wrote a letter to the commandant claiming that bastardisation was adversely affecting the Fourth Class cadets' academic performance. He wrote that the cadets often appeared 'dazed, shocked, tense, and very unhappy – conditions such as would render any form of instruction less effective'. An internal Board of Inquiry Report was subsequently leaked to Canberra journalist Maxwell Newton. His inflammatory reports led to the Minister for the Army, Phillip Lynch, establishing a Committee of Inquiry under the chairmanship of ACT Supreme Court Justice R. W. Fox. The Fox Report was tabled in Federal Parliament on 12 June 1970. It concluded:

> We are emphatic that the conduct, which has come to be called 'bastardisation', must be banned. It is senseless and degrading. It is not countenanced elsewhere in the army and there is no place for it at the Royal Military College.

During his torrid first six months at Duntroon, Cos did what most cadets did who successfully endured the hazing. He copped it. He followed Duntroon's unofficial mock-Latin motto: *nil bastardo carborundum* – 'Don't let the bastards grind you down'.

The experience stretched him far more than he had thought. He handled the academic side with relative ease but the physical side was different. Cadets had to run a mile in six minutes, no mean feat, and one for which Cos was not naturally predisposed. Nor was he a natural swimmer, as Mike McDermott observed:

> He lived at bloody Bronte but he couldn't swim. We had swimming tests, in full uniform – and the safety device they used was a basketball. If somebody got into trouble, they threw him the basketball and he hung onto it. By this stage I'd worked out he couldn't swim. We had to swim a hundred metres in our jungle greens. He's standing on the blocks, and he's sweating. But that's where he showed guts.

They blow the whistle, Next group, go! Cos goes down about eleven foot. I could see his eyes coming up. He splutters, 'Throw me the ball!' And I've got the ball and they're saying, 'Throw him the ball!' And I'm saying, 'No, bugger him'. And eventually some bloke wrestled me to the ground and gave him the ball. I think it took Cos some time to see the humour.

A couple of years later we were at a swimming pool and he dived in and boom, boom, boom, he swam to the other end. He'd taught himself. That's what I admired about him.

Cos regarded the challenges as tests of character, drawing on all his powers of resilience and the support of his mates, and pushed on.

Mike McDermott saw Cos' stoic endurance as an example of his determination to overcome any obstacles and stay the course:

The physical side and the administrative side were a challenge for him but he overcame that and succeeded. The academic side was a breeze for him. He could have got the Queen's Medal (for Dux of the College) I would say. He had a tremendous potential but he didn't always meet that potential because of all the other things he wanted to do at Duntroon – like having a beer, going to football training and mucking round in general. And he wasn't studying and applying himself to his study.

Cos was also sustained in the early days at Duntroon by the regular flow of five- and six-page letters he received from his mother, updating him on family affairs and the world outside. Like other sympathetic parents, Ellen also included the occasional box of his favourite foods, such as a fruitcake or some salted crackers.

★ ★ ★

During his second year, Cos' beloved grandad, Bob Henrys, died. He learned the news after an especially harrowing episode of bastardisation, as Mike McDermott recalled:

> The night before, some senior cadets had got Cos into a room and they were shouting at him and bastardising him pretty solidly. The next day, after he'd been up all night, he came in and said, 'Shit, I'm stuffed.' I said, 'You lie down behind your bed. Stick your security box up against the heater and go to sleep and I'll cover for you.' He said, 'Oh, okay, thanks,' and he made himself a little bed and went to sleep.
>
> A little while later these senior blokes came running around, 'Where's your mate, Cosgrove?' They followed me over to the drying room and they said, 'Somebody's looking for your mate Cosgrove.' I asked whether it was the duty officer and they said, 'Yes, how did you know that?' I said, 'Somebody already told me . . . Look, all I can tell you, is he's been to see the padre.' They immediately

jumped to conclusions. (Some people used the padre as a conduit to the commandant and they would go and say, 'These blokes are bastardising me.') These blokes chasing Cos nearly shat blue light.

Mike played it for all it was worth. When Cos' assailants found out about his grandfather they did the decent thing and eased off on his hazing for a while. The loss hit Cos hard but it also stiffened his resolve and he was able to draw on Bob's spirit to continue his resistance. A little later, Cos received some far happier news. His father had been promoted from Warrant Officer First Class to Captain. Cos was extremely proud that his father had risen from digger to win a commission. It was another incentive for him to emulate his father by completing his course at Duntroon and earn his own commission.

As the bastardisation eased, Cos was able to appreciate some of Duntroon's more enlightening and uplifting experiences. He grew to appreciate its grounds and its beautiful buildings, many of them heritage-listed, and he soaked up its special aura. A lifetime later he would write affectionately in the introduction to Vivien Dwyer's beautiful book, *Duntroon: an Artist's Impression*, that it was: '. . . a place of grim purpose and hard edges, where Australian men and women are trained to lead and fight wars and win . . . a place of rich beauty and history, of timeless military liturgy, of humanity and warmth'.

Cos' greatest pleasures at Duntroon revolved around sport, principally rugby and cricket. (When he was Chief of the Defence Force, he would lyrically reflect on his rugby career in a Sydney University luncheon, 'I was the sort of loose-forward who lay contentedly on the bottom of a ruck, composing sonnets on the one hand and, on another plane, contemplating applying the squirrel grip to an opponent.') It was sport that helped to change his life as a cadet. One day in Third Class, he and Mike McDermott were mucking around near 'The Square' when a voice boomed out from 200 metres away, 'You two fellas, Cosgrove and McDermott, get over to my office now!' It was one of the staff instructors. He was also the coach of the senior football teams. The news was good. 'You two are going to senior football.' This meant they would move up from the under-19 rugby teams to the senior grades. It also meant that after games they would go out and have a few beers with the senior class men. Cos' confidence on the rugby field grew and he won recognition as a feared breakaway, a marauding loose-forward who tackled and took the ball up with fierce determination. He also found success in the boxing ring, winning the light-heavyweight title at the college with a stunning knockout punch that poleaxed his opponent in the final. It was another step along the road to acceptance.

As he progressed up the classes, Cos began to appreciate the quality of the men who taught him, as he would later acknowledge in a speech as Chief of the Defence Force:

[The Royal Military College was] . . . perhaps the most critical influence in developing my leadership skills. Our instructors all had seen active service, and more than a couple had decorations for gallantry.

There were some very distinguished soldiers on the staff, and we looked up to them, and modelled ourselves as leaders on those we admired. We were given every opportunity, in our barracks, on the sporting field, and in our training to develop our leadership potential. We were constantly being taught, observed and assessed. We learned leadership in any number of ways from any number of teachers and mentors so that by the time we had graduated we had a clear vision of the sort of leader we wanted to be, and of the leadership style we would adopt.

It soon became evident that Cos' class, which would graduate as the class of 1968, was very talented. It boasted a number of outstanding individuals and a body of high-quality officers. The class went on to achieve the rare feat of producing three generals and many who later rose to top-level positions. On average, a graduating class would produce perhaps one general.

But observers in 1968 would have been hard pressed to nominate Cos as a likely general, let alone future Chief of the Defence Force – especially if they had seen him on his twenty-first birthday on 28 July of that year. It was the custom that those with a birthday would be given a special cold-bath treatment to celebrate. It was in the dead of Canberra's winter and Cos very sensibly tried to anticipate and defuse the ordeal. He approached his mate Mike McDermott to dissuade any likely celebrations. Big mistake.

When Cos returned from the mess, about 40 Fourth Class cadets gleefully repaid his earlier hazing attentions by grabbing him, stripping him, shoving him in a cold bath and then tying him naked to a steel bed and putting him out in the snow that was blanketing the terrace. His 'mate' McDermott arrived, wearing a balaclava and a greatcoat to protect himself from the cold, sipping a warming coffee.

> I said, 'Mate, this is bloody uncivilised, you being out here.' By now Cos is trying to break his ropes without success. The Fourth Class blokes had fled so I untied his ropes a little and I walked inside and I locked the door.
>
> Suddenly, through the door . . . Wooshka! . . . came this wild, white apparition. The whole door crashed down. And he's running along the corridor after these Fourth Classes. They're fleeing for their lives.
>
> We put in a lost and damaged report on the door, explaining that he and I were out having a cup of coffee and we stumbled, fell and hit the door and the door came off its hinges. It got down to the quartermaster and he said, 'I will not believe a word that these two villains say. Members to pay!'

As they prepared for their graduation parade, the hierarchy of the class of 1968 was evident. Grant Chaseling was appointed the Battalion Sergeant Major (BSM) and won the Sword of Honour as the top cadet and Colin Sanders won the Queen's Medal as the top academic achiever. (Ironically, neither would have life-long careers in the army.) Under the BSM was the Battalion Quartermaster Sergeant (BQS), and each of the four companies had an underofficer in charge of them. Each of those companies had a quartermaster sergeant and each company had three platoons led by a sergeant. Cos and Mike McDermott were appointed as two of those sergeants. It was a position of considerable pride for Cos but not one signalling that his superiors yet recognised that he was destined for the highest echelons of command. Clearly, this hierarchy should never be taken too seriously because each of the three generals who would later emerge from Cos' class – Cos, Peter Dunn and Michael O'Brien – was a platoon sergeant on their final parade at Duntroon.

Perhaps a more accurate indication of Cos' potential was revealed when he was assigned to his first choice of corps or infantry, at graduation. It was a keenly sought appointment because the Vietnam War was in full swing and it held out the chance of putting theoretical training into real practice.

Lieutenant Peter Cosgrove wore the shiny new pips on his epaulettes with great pride. He could look back on his experience at Duntroon with satisfaction. He had met the challenges and he had come to appreciate the college motto, 'Doctrina vim promovet' ('Knowledge promotes strength'). It would serve him throughout his life.

THE
GREASY POLE 5

It was a far more worldly-wise Lieutenant Peter
Cosgrove who returned to Australia in late 1970 after his
tour of duty in Vietnam than the young man who
headed there 12 months earlier. He returned to take up a
posting with the Methods of Instruction Team at Ingleburn, outside Sydney. His Vietnam experiences had left a
deep impression.

> Vietnam changed me. It made me a lot more of a
> serious person and perhaps a lot more confident.
> I had an early test of what I was made of and I
> came out okay. I had no illusions that I was God's

gift, but I became very aware of the very serious side of soldiering – as a life-and-death issue.

During Cos' time in Vietnam, the Australian public's view of the war had also undergone a complete about-turn. In 1965, when he had entered Duntroon, polls showed a clear majority support for the nation's involvement in the war. By the end of 1969, while he was in harm's way leading his platoon on active service, public opinion had swung the other way as Australians back home were confronted with casualty lists, body bags and gruesome nightly TV news images. The anti-war moratorium movement was at its height. Shortly after he returned home, more than 100,000 demonstrators marched in Melbourne. The groundswell of anti-war sentiment was forcing the Gorton Government's hand.

Cos escaped any personal abuse on his return home. He didn't suffer the indignities heaped on some veterans on their return, like those who had symbolic red paint thrown at them during their welcome-home parade or others who were refused admission to their local RSL because they were told by World War II vets that 'Vietnam wasn't a real war, just a police action.' Cos recalled only being 'taken to task once or twice by people from my own age group from other walks of life'. Perhaps it was because he was cocooned by a family imbued with army traditions and was embraced as a regular soldier into the army structure with all its support systems. Cos has never regretted his service in Vietnam. He has always separated the morality or otherwise of Australia's commitment to the war from his duty as a soldier to serve his country as directed.

In February 1971, Cos heard the news that he'd been awarded the Military Cross (MC) for his bravery in leading his platoon on Operation Jack in Vietnam. It was a source of immense pride for his father. The MC is awarded to commissioned officers of Major or below for gallant and distinguished services in battle. It has a proud history, having been established in December 1915. It has adorned the breasts of many brave men in all conflicts since World War I and commands respect from armed forces around the world.

A month after Cos heard the news, William McMahon ousted Gorton as Liberal Party Leader and was sworn in as Australian Prime Minister. In August that year McMahon announced the final withdrawal of troops from Vietnam. On 2 December 1972, McMahon was soundly defeated by Labor's Gough Whitlam in the 'It's time' election.

Many years later, Cos would recast his views on Australia's involvement in the Vietnam War and conclude that, overall, it was a mistake. Despite this, the conflict provided the opportunity for a young warrior of obvious promise to show his mettle and to demonstrate his leadership potential. As he would do many times in his storied career, first Cos took the opportunity with enthusiasm and clear purpose.

Without question, a Military Cross was a career boost for a young officer and it opened doors that might not have been otherwise available. The award helped to place Cos in the list of potential candidates for one of the most sought-after postings for a young subaltern: aide de camp (ADC) to the Governor-General. His Military Cross was a tick in his favour but it was Cos' personality, presentation skills and intellect that won him the nod from the patrician Sir Paul Hasluck. Cosgrove took advantage of the opportunities presented to him.

The seventeenth Governor-General of Australia, Paul Meernaa Caedwalla Hasluck, was a rare breed in Australian politics. He was a deep-thinking intellectual, with an academic background and a literary bent. He was born and educated in Western Australia, where his early years were split between literary journalism and university lecturing. In 1941 he joined the Department of External Affairs and after the war he wrote the civilian volumes of the Official History of Australia's role in World War II. In 1949, he entered federal politics as a Liberal candidate for a Perth electorate and soon won ministerial office under the Menzies Government, first as Minister for External Territories, then as Minister for Defence and finally as Minister for External Affairs, a post he held during the early years of our involvement in the Vietnam War, for which he was an enthusiastic proponent. As Minister for External Affairs, Hasluck crossed swords many times with the rapier-witted Leader of the Opposition, Gough Whitlam. On one famous occasion in 1965, Hasluck provoked Whitlam to throw a glass of water at him in the House by calling him '. . . one of the filthiest objects ever to come into this chamber'.

When Prime Minister Harold Holt drowned at Cheviot Beach in Victoria in December 1967, 64-year-old Hasluck threw his hat into the ring in the subsequent battle for the leadership. He did it largely to stymie the run of William McMahon but both lost out to John Gorton. In turn, Gorton decided to eliminate any further challenge from Hasluck by appointing him Governor-General in 1969.

By the time Cos took up his position as Hasluck's ADC, the Governor-General was an established, opinionated observer of Australian and world affairs. By observation and conversation at Yarralumla, Cos learned the not-so-gentle art of diplomacy and political awareness. He shared a deep love of history with Hasluck and relished his chances to listen, learn and debate with the old hand. The two also shared a passion for cricket and would chat about the great game's nuances over a nightcap after the official day was done.

Cos would often tell friends that his most dangerous duty was ensuring that the Governor-General's makings for his cocktail were laid out on the cocktail tray each night. 'You had to get that right. If you got that wrong, now you were in deep trouble.'

As a young unmarried officer (a prerequisite for the job), Cos attended functions, luncheons, dinners and occasions at Yarralumla at a glittering array of venues with the good and the great and the powerful from around Australia and across the world. It was a wonderful opportunity to listen, to watch and to soak up the atmosphere of the powerful and the power-brokers from Australia and overseas at work. He also observed, and was observed by, those from the highest echelons of the services, whom he represented as one of its bright young stars on the rise.

The experience gave Cos a concentrated course in political sensitivity. It would prove a fine grounding for many of his future appointments. His success in the role gave his superiors confidence that the young tearaway platoon commander could handle himself in the sometimes hazardous world of politics. He also learned more of the theoretical and practical operation of the division of power. It was Hasluck who clarified the rarely appreciated role of the Governor-General as the titular head, or Commander-in-Chief, of Australia's armed forces:

The exercise by the Governor-General of the 'command-in-chief' of the armed forces is qualified by a number of statutes of the Australian Parliament and the regulations made under them. The constitutional provision means, however, that unless the Constitution is amended the command-in-chief cannot be placed elsewhere.

Parliament can legislate to provide for the administration of the defence system and for making military appointments in the defence forces but it cannot vest the command-in-chief in any other person or body. This ensures that civil administration and civil control of those forces will remain and be exercised by a Governor-General acting with the advice of ministers.

The Chief of the Defence Force (CDF) commands the

daily administration and operation of the services. Through the Executive Council, the Governor-General appoints the CDF and the Chiefs of the Army, Navy and Air Force and commissions their officers.

Cos also learned a valuable lesson in the way Hasluck refused to allow his personal feelings to interfere with the duties of his high office. For example, despite their personal animosity, Hasluck's relations with Gough Whitlam – after he was elected as the new Prime Minister in December 1972 – were impeccable.

After his year at Yarralumla, Cos looked forward to his next posting, as a temporary captain, to 5RAR (the 'Tigers', 5th Battalion Royal Australian Regiment) based at Holsworthy, in Sydney's west. 5RAR was then commanded by Colonel Kevin Newman and had a fine record in both the Korean and Vietnam wars. Its battle honours included Long Tan, Coral and Balmoral, three of the key actions in Vietnam. Captain Peter Cosgrove MC took up his posting as second in command of Delta Company 5RAR. Colleagues remember that Cos brought with him a quiet confidence born of his Vietnam service. To some he still had a bit of the tear-away about him but he impressed many with his capacity for leadership and his clear understanding of the power of the various support groups available to the infantry, another direct benefit of his active service. He showed sound tactical skills in the field and an ability to bring all available arms into the environment, whether it be artillery or aviation.

Around this time there was a shift in strategic

approach by Australia's armed forces towards a philosophy based around the defence of continental Australia,
together with a politically inspired downsizing of the
national service input into the army. It also meant a
substantial change in emphasis in training and exercises,
from jungle training to working in the desert and other
open spaces.

One of the first operations in which Cos found
himself involved was 'Operation Dark Moon' in the
outback desert. Sleeping by day and operating at night in
an environment a world away from the lush jungle-green
humidity of Vietnam, Cos adapted quickly and his work
soon caught the eye of his CO. Colonel Newman
appointed Cos as his Adjutant – essentially the CO's
right-hand man.

Kevin Newman saw what those who took in the
young Cos at first glance sometimes missed. He was an
extremely clever young man with a great capacity for
work and an ability to learn quickly and on his feet. His
rambunctious, even reckless, actions on the rugby paddock
led many observers to dismiss him as a footy boofhead.
Newman was the first of many of Cos' subsequent bosses
who recognised his singular clarity of thought: his ability
to simplify complex problems, to stick to the point and to
clearly articulate the problem and the solution. Even at
this early stage of his career, Cos was developing the ability
to express himself both on paper and in person. It would
be the foundation of the skills that would allow him to
master the 20-second media grab that would endear him
to reporters in East Timor almost 30 years later.

Above all, Cos had an instinctive understanding of the need for leaders to be communicators. He also possessed the rare ability to be able to feel comfortable in people's company and to be inclusive. The legacy of this particular ability is the number of people who count him as a friend.

From the time that Cos took over as Adjutant, he had a positive impact on the operation of the battalion and was an effective conduit to his CO. One of his colleagues at the time remembers how Cos impressed observers with his organisation of a presentation at one of his early audits groups, where the battalion commander gives his formal orders to the company commanders, all of the supported arms, transports groups, etcetera for an operation. In a room chockfull of 40 or 50 officers, Kevin Newman gave a captivating exposition of the plan of action, reeling off grid references, timings and intricate details with a single note. 'Right, A company, your tasks are as follows . . . you will rendezvous at 22.45 hours at grid reference 687 216, you will proceed to secure the feature at grid reference . . .'

It went on like clockwork for 40 minutes to the growing appreciation of the assembly. Nobody, except Newman and Cos, the man who had orchestrated the performance, noticed the intelligence sergeant outside the window who was feverishly flipping through a series of large sheets of cardboard with all the details on them.

Cos has always understood the importance of the theatre of presentation. Not only would he do the work in preparing the data for inclusion for his presentation, he would work equally hard at the presentation itself.

★ ★ ★

In December 1973, as part of the army's downsizing, 5RAR was amalgamated with 7RAR to form 5-7RAR, a mechanised battalion. Cos was promoted to Major and appointed back to Delta Company, this time as its commander. It was the continuation of the impressive body of commands that would characterise his career.

★ ★ ★

It was while he was at Holsworthy that Cos met the woman who would become the love of his life. As those who have served there will readily admit, Holsworthy could never lay claim to be the epicentre of Sydney's social life. But it has always held a fond place in Cos' heart for the role it played in allowing him to meet a beautiful and vivacious 27-year-old from Sydney's southern suburbs. Lynne Elizabeth Payne was six months younger than Cos and a building society branch man-ager. She had been brought to the officers' mess by a mutual friend, Terry Smith, who was serving in the Army Reserve. Cos was immediately smitten and they began courting. Cos recalled his first impression of Lynne to Andrew Denton on ABC TV's *Enough Rope*:

> Oh, wonderful, wonderful, attractive, a vibrant glamorous woman that I thought, Wow. And then later on I thought, But if she's keen on me she's

going to need to like the army. And I thought, Well, that will be tricky. But she turned out to be able to tolerate the army tolerably well.

After he met Lynne, Cos immediately rang Mike McDermott. 'Oh, mate. She's great. Wait till you meet her.' Lynne lived in the Sutherland Shire, where her father was a butcher. Cos ended up spending a lot of time on the roads between Holsworthy, Lynne's home and the seemingly endless series of exercises, training and administrative duties that characterised his work. Their second date was an army function so Lynne knew what she was in for from the start. In January 1976, having by now been posted as an Officer Instructor of Tactics to the Infantry Centre at Singleton in northern New South Wales, Cos proposed to Lynne from a pay phone box outside the mess. Cos later admitted he'd attended a candlelit dinner at the officers' mess and was overwhelmed by the happy couples surrounding him. He ran out of coins halfway through the call but persuaded a sympathetic operator to allow the romantic exchange to continue.

Terry Smith and Mike McDermott were in the bridal party when Cos and Lynne married at Cos' alma mater, Waverley College, on 17 December 1976 and held their reception at the Australian Golf Club.

Lynne has always said she went into their partnership with her eyes wide open. Luckily for Cos, she was prepared to accept the considerable disruption and discomfort involved in a military marriage, as she confirmed in Gina Lennox's *Forged by War*.

What has helped is that I am one of the last of the dinosaurs: I was very prepared to put my life into my husband's career, and being married to a career soldier has given me a tremendously varied life.

And just as well, because unlike the navy, where wives can settle with their family at a base while their husbands travel, army wives are subjected to a relentless series of moves. In Lynne Cosgrove's case it meant moving more than 20 times, including three overseas postings. Each time it was Lynne who was left to pick up the pieces after the dislocation: to reassemble their home; to make new friends and social connections; and, in due course, to settle the children into a new school.

Lynne had barely adjusted to married life before she became pregnant with their first child. Stephen John Cosgrove was born on 9 March 1978, shortly before the family headed off to the United States where Cos, now Major Cosgrove, was posted to the US Marine Corps Staff College in Quantico, Virginia. This was a very significant posting, signalling that Cos' career was well on track. In each cohort (or group of similarly experienced and qualified, and therefore competing, officers travelling through the ranks) of perhaps 80 officers who are to attend staff college, a handful is chosen to attend overseas staff colleges in Britain, the United States, India, Germany, France, Canada and others. Of these, the three key postings are to Camberley, the British Staff College, and to Quantico and Fort Leavenworth, in the United States. That Cos was appointed to Quantico, the highly coveted staff academic centre for the US Marine Corps, showed that his superiors regarded him as having the capacity and the potential for considerable further advancement. It is generally accepted that an infantry officer who has been to Quantico has an excellent chance of becoming a battalion commander, one of the key goals of a combat soldier. At the massive military centre at Quantico, Cos was exposed to state-of-the-art practices in amphibious warfare and coordinated combat operations, knowledge he would later put to effective use in East Timor.

While Cos was expanding his knowledge, Lynne was coping as a first-time mother in a new apartment in a foreign land. To her great credit, she had little difficulty in establishing a network of new friends and nestling into the military community there. One of the constant comments from people who know her is that Lynne has wonderful social skills, an ability to mix with people from all walks of life and to form and maintain friendships. From the beginning, Lynne and Cos' marriage was based on friendship, mutual respect and love. This partnership gave Cos a rock-solid base from which he could expand his career.

Shortly after the Cosgroves returned to Sydney from Quantico, their second child, Philip William Cosgrove, was born on 17 October 1979. Peter had moved to Headquarters, Field Force Command at Victoria Barracks, just around the corner from where he was born in Paddington. Lynne once again held the fort when, just before Christmas 1979, Cos was sent to

Rhodesia as part of the Commonwealth team observing the first free elections for the new republic of Zimbabwe. Lynne was left with Stephen, under two, and Philip, two months old. Fortunately, Cos was only away for a couple of months before returning to Victoria Barracks, where the family enjoyed a rare period in the one place. Their third son, David Michael Cosgrove, was born on 20 December 1982.

★ ★ ★

In 1983 Cos was promoted to Lieutenant Colonel and given the command that he'd always wished for: the 1st Battalion Royal Australian Regiment. Cos showed how importantly he regarded the appointment by preparing himself, both mentally and physically. He went on a rigorous fitness campaign and trimmed down to a fighting weight of around 80 kilograms, a substantial drop from his bulk at Holsworthy and Victoria Barracks. He lost so much weight that some of his contemporaries remember he looked a little grey and drawn. But he knew what he needed to do. 1RAR was based in the tropical heat of Townsville and it formed part of the recently established Operational Deployment Force (ODF), the group that would be first called on for any combat operations. Cos and his men had to pass regular ODF checks before they could assume the necessary short-degree notice.

As a battalion commander, Cos was able to demonstrate his all-round command skills. He revealed to both his men and his superiors that he was far more than an infantry commander. He exhibited an outstanding ability to co-ordinate the various elements under his command and adroitly manoeuvred and deployed his artillery and aviation support. He showed particular capacity in working with artillery and won acclaim for his work with 'danger-close' artillery. His organisational skills were a feature of his battalion's exercises, in which he played the role of the orchestra conductor.

Typically, a training exercise would involve the 1500-strong battalion group and it would start at 4 am and finish late the following afternoon. It required exceptional precision, often in 42-degree heat and sweltering humidity. On one occasion, the battalion was arriving back after bashing its way in full combat kit through the heat of the day. It was in textbook order – the gun battery, all the companies and then, right at the end, the small group of a dozen or so battalion headquarters staff, all belting along into the setting sun. Cos brought up the rear. Encouraging his troops right on to the parade ground, he arrived almost to the second – with the entire team intact. With a flourish, he reported to the brigadier that the whole battalion group, 1500 men, with all their equipment and all their stores, were all fit and ready to go. It was Cos the soldier, with a slice of the performer, at his best. And he was loving it. It would be the fittest he'd ever been but the challenge of the command brought out the best in him and allowed him to conquer his propensity to stack on the kilos. He was able to set an example to some of the fittest of his troops – at that stage some of the fittest in the army.

★ ★ ★

Cos impressed his superiors and subordinates with his ability to communicate, his clarity of purpose and his determination and competitiveness. This latter characteristic was sometimes overshadowed by his bonhomie but it was ever-present, and was best illustrated by his attitude to sport. Up until his appointment as CO of 1RAR, Cos had continued to play services sport competitively, especially cricket and rugby. As CO, he funnelled his competitive urges into his unit's teams. For example, during a regimental gun race competition, where various units' artillery teams vied for superiority in disassembling their guns, taking them over various obstacles and then reassembling them, Cos, prepared an area within the bowels of 1RAR's base so that his team could train away from their competitors' prying eyes. He also impressed them with his technical knowledge in helping them with tips. It didn't matter which of the unit's dozen sporting teams was in action, Cos was there to support them and to do whatever was necessary, teasing out every issue so that every member was in the right place at the right time, even if he had to travel 100 kilometres to play the game. As one contemporary said, 'Cos was very competitive for the battalion, very competitive in exercises and as cunning as a shithouse rat in doing it.'

On another occasion, when 1RAR played the role of the enemy in an exercise in the Pilbara, his tactics such as hitting and running like guerrillas, using small white Toyotas and having troops dress as farm girls, sorely tested what was effectively the main body of the Operational Deployment Force. Cos lived the role of the opponent to the full and won considerable respect for his work in the field, not least among his own troops. One subordinate summed it up:

> Peter was truly revered by the troops in 1RAR, they were proud of him. And whereas others tended to drive the diggers, he led them. Not that that meant he was everybody's mate but by firm, fair and friendly leadership.

Enlightened by his experiences in combat in Vietnam, Cos knew that assiduous training would prepare his troops for the actions they would be required to take but that they still would have to deal with 'the fog of war' should they go into combat. He tried to prepare his troops for this eventuality by encouraging his experienced officers and NCOs to pass on their knowledge to the young diggers.

Cos understood the value of what the army calls the regimental system where the RSM of a battalion works as a vital and close colleague of the CO, the company sergeant major works with his company commander, the experienced NCOs help their junior officers and so on down the line to corporals helping their young diggers, even experienced diggers helping newcomers.

This was the message and the experience that Cos constantly communicated to his company commanders, to his platoon commanders, to his NCOs in officer training, all the while passing on the principles involved and the lessons learned rather than his individual experiences.

★ ★ ★

While Cos held sway with the diggers, Lynne came into her own in the vital role of the CO's wife. In addition to running the home during the long hours when Cos was occupied with operational duties, Lynne shouldered the complementary leadership role with the battalion's families. There is often a tortuous symmetry between the two roles: the CO's work results in the soldiers being kept away from their families, so the CO's wife is often left to pick up the pieces. She tends to be the support lifeline for the tragedies that often haunt military life: injuries and deaths and family break-ups and tensions. Lynne won wide acclaim for her compassion and capacity.

★ ★ ★

When Cos was CO of 1RAR, his friend Michael Keating, who had graduated a year ahead of him at Duntroon, was commanding 2/4th Battalion in Townsville and building a fine reputation as an infantryman. To many observers at that time, Cos, Keating and Peter Abigail, who graduated the year after Cos at Duntroon, represented the new wave of army leadership. The men had developed in the period after the establishment of the Operational Deployment Force (ODF). During this time the army had become leaner, meaner and more austere, more 'operationally focused' than the image of the service held by the generation ahead of them, led by outstanding men like John Sanderson, Frank Hickling and John Huntley. The old breed's experience and training (two of them were engineers, one of them was in intelligence) saw them more inclined to use bureaucratic processes in their approach to combat readiness. The new breed leaned to a more capable, light strike force along the lines of the Operational Deployment Force. They had all served in Vietnam and all had been commanded by the highly respected Murray Blake, who had won a Military Cross during the Battle of Coral in Vietnam and was the commander of the 3rd Brigade when Cos, Keating and Abigail were battalion commanders there. Blake would go on to serve as Land Commander in the early 1990s. Cos, Keating and Abigail were destined to contend with each other for the army's highest posts.

Cos didn't quite finish his full two years as a battalion commander because in 1984 he was posted as an exchange instructor to the British Army Staff college at Camberley in Surrey, England, another keenly sought appointment and one that generally signals a bright future.

★ ★ ★

Lynne dutifully packed up the three boys – all under six – and followed. It turned out to be a wonderful experience for both of them. Cos served as one of Camberley's directing staff, one of the instructors who lead discussion groups and tutor, assess and mark students. The posting requires the appointee to be a capable ambassador and is considered a valuable element in the preparation of senior command officers. As he did in Quantico, Cos made valuable future connections at Camberley with officers from around the world who had exchange arrangements there. These friendships and links would serve him well in East Timor and in his later roles as Chief of the Army and Defence Force.

Nineteen eighty-five started with a flourish when, in January, Cos was awarded the Order of Australia (AM) in recognition for his work as commander of 1RAR. Later that year his world was shaken when his beloved father died. John Cosgrove had retired from the army in 1975 after 38 years and had become the Secretary-Manager of the Waverley Bowling Club in Sydney. He was at the club when he suffered a heart attack and died on 7 August, aged 69. John was buried alongside his father in the Catholic section of Waverley cemetery. In spite of his many absences on duty, John and Cos had established a close and affectionate relationship which grew with their shared experiences over the years. Cos always credited his father with providing him with the role model that persuaded him to choose a career in the military and often described him as a 'kind and loving father' who was seemingly unaffected by his war experiences.

In 1987 Cos continued his advancement when he was appointed as Military Assistant to the Chief of the General Staff before attending the Joint Services Staff College the following year. Then he worked at Headquarters Australian Defence Force (ADF) and as Director of Combat Development at Army Office before, in January 1990, he was made Commandant of the Infantry Centre and Director of Infantry. It was a role Cos relished as it gave him yet another command, one that allowed him to be involved directly with the digger and gave him opportunities to appreciate the digger's special spirit.

The digger is to some extent always mildly pushing the envelope. I can remember when I was the Director of Infantry and I was watching a whole group of infantry soldiers in the Duke of Gloucester Cup. It was the section competition and they were going through some very arduous military tests.

They'd been hard at it for days, all trying to outdo each other on behalf of the infantry battalion. Each battalion of the Royal Australian Regiment provided a section and they were just punishing themselves to be the best. It was late on the last day of the competition and I'd brought a whole lot of venerable old retired officers by Land Rover up this extraordinarily steep bush track, one where you get sunburn on the roof of your mouth walking up it.

The Land Rover was groaning its way up in low gear past these sweating soldiers who were climbing this hill. At the top we popped out of the vehicle fresh and we watched these kids struggle the last few metres across the finish line. There was some kid with a machine gun and a very heavy load plodding up this hill. He looked up and he saw me and suddenly assumed this very worried expression and looked at me and said, 'Oh, hello, Sir, how are you?' I said, 'I'm all right, soldier,' and he said, 'You're not tired or anything are you, Sir, because this hill's very steep.' I said, 'No, I'm actually not as tired as you, mate, so do carry on.' That was typical, the irreverence and at the end of the gruelling test this guy still had a spark of humour left in him.

In 1992 Cos was promoted to Brigadier and assumed command of the 6th Brigade, based in Brisbane. Two years later, he extended his overseas experience with a stint at the Indian National Defence College in 1994. This was an eye-opening introduction to the massive Indian Army. It is the third largest armed force in the world, with more than a million active troops and 800,000 reservists. Cos studied its special needs and methods. He spent hair-raising hours in choppers at 7000 metres in Kashmir where the air is so thin that, even with four blades, the rotors are grasping for lift. He observed the way the Indians handled the long-running tensions over Kashmir with their Pakistani neighbours, and he extended his circle of influence and his contacts with military leaders from the sub-continent and Asia.

On his return in 1995 Cos was appointed the Commandant of the Australian Defence Warfare Centre at Williamstown, New South Wales, where he took over as the army's representative at the centre following a stint there by the navy.

In April 1995 Cos' mum, Ellen, died aged 74. She had been a tireless worker for the Army Wives' Association, for which she served as its long-time honorary secretary, even after John retired. She was remembered for her energy and wit and for her selfless service. She was always the one who did the real work: organising functions and speakers, even putting out the chairs and the name-tags and folding the napkins. She was always in the background but never short of an intelligent opinion. She formed the spiritual and practical backbone of her family and was an invaluable sounding-board to Cos while he was growing up and throughout his career. He lost a friend and a kindred soul with her passing.

During his time at the Warfare Centre, Cos embarked on the enormous task of revising the written doctrine of the three arms of the defence's forces: army, navy and air force. This involved a complete rewriting of all the technical guidebooks on which the forces based their training and operating procedures. Cos drew on his considerable communication and English language skills to simplify and add professional and technical value to the material, some of which had not been substantially revised since World War II. The task enabled him to draw on his strategic planning ability to integrate the doctrine with the changes in the way the forces were approaching the art of campaigning. Years of involvement at the operational level, since Vietnam, had meant the Australian

Defence Force (ADF) was good at little, but not so good at big. Cos set about integrating the doctrinal changes needed to enable the ADF to move from the tactical level, as in Vietnam, where Australia had set areas of operation within the overall prosecution of the war, to the strategic or operational level, where it could successfully handle the art of campaigning.

Cos was well prepared for the task. He had commanded at the platoon, company, battalion and brigade levels and had undergone a continuous stream of national and international staff studies in leadership, planning, operations and administration. These experiences would serve as a wonderful preparation for his involvement in East Timor, the first chance the ADF had to substantially test its ability to conduct a major campaign.

Even during his command periods, Cos always had a grudging appreciation for the doctrine writers and analysts with whom he came into contact: those whose job it was to record the results of exercises and apply the lessons learned from them against the existing doctrine. He often used to turn around, see the note-takers and exclaim with a grin, 'They also serve who only stand and perve!'

During this time Cos fought a series of running battles with the navy and air force, persuading them of the merit of the changes to doctrine he was proposing. Throughout the conflicts he kept his larrikin humour. It often emerged without warning. At one stage, Cos had become concerned at the number of his staff who were travelling by pushbike along the dangerous roads to and from the Warfare Centre. His warnings went largely unheeded and his worst fears were realised when one of his Majors was hit by a massive beef truck. The impact imbedded the bike into this man's upper leg. Three transfusions later, his survival was touch and go. Eventually, when Cos received the news that he would make it, he said, 'Thank God! Tell him I've been telling him to stick that bike of his up his arse for the last couple of years and he did!'

Things came full circle at the end of 1996 when Cos was appointed Commandant of Duntroon. One of the first things he did was to look up his student files. That's when he discovered that he hadn't imagined the tough time he had as a Fourth Class cadet: he held the record for extra drills for his class.

It was yet another move for the family but this time the disruption was more than compensated for by the elegant surroundings into which they moved. In the 30 years since he attended the College, Cos had formed some clear views on positive initiatives he planned to introduce. One was dear to his heart. Sport was no longer compulsory for cadets. Cos passionately believed in the individual and team benefits resulting from sport and he re-established it in the curriculum.

He also set about implementing a common approach to officer training for both reserve and regular candidates. He programmed various modules for reserve officers so that every officer in the Australian Army graduated from the parade ground of the Royal Military College. He watched with pride as parents, family and community bore witness to graduation ceremonies in front of a peer group that includes the reserves, the regulars and the ADF Academy.

A keen student of digger history, Cos well knew the friction that developed in World War II between the AIF, or regulars, and the Militia, the reserves. The AIF dismissed the Militia as chockos, or chocolate soldiers, who would melt in the heat of battle. It wasn't until they fought shoulder-to-shoulder at the turning-point battle at Isurava on the Kokoda Track in 1942 that the barriers were broken down. Cos knew the importance of all members feeling confident that they were part of the bigger defence family. Perhaps most importantly, the parents and families of the graduates were enthusiastic supporters and beneficiaries.

By late 1997, observers were looking at the various candidates for the army's top jobs. As Commandant of Duntroon Cos reported to Training Command, which was commanded by his old mate, now Major General Mike Keating. Peter Abigail would soon be promoted to Major General so both he and Mike Keating now seemed to have the inside running for the higher appointments.

There may have been times during his period as Commandant of Duntroon when it crossed Cos' mind that he may have missed his chance for the top jobs. By that stage he'd had three commands as a brigadier – the Infantry Centre, 6th Brigade and Duntroon – and had not yet been promoted to Major General. Sometimes this was a signal that a career had stalled. But, not for the last time, Cos caught a late wave. In March 1998 he was promoted to Major General and made Commander of 1st Division and the Deployable Joint Force Head- quarters in Brisbane. Later that year Mike Keating was given the Chief Operations position in Canberra (controlling the operations bunker in the ADF Command Centre under the Russell Offices). Peter Abigail was given his second command as Major General by being made Deputy Chief of the Army. All three men were now Major Generals but Abigail on his second appoint- ment at that rank and Mike Keating on his third were still in the box seats. Many outside observers, seeing the age at which Cos was promoted to the most junior general's position, were tipping that he'd be lucky to advance much further beyond that appointment. As Cos moved into his second year as Commander of the Deployable Joint Force in Brisbane, the events which would irreparably change his life began to take shape to his north.

THE LION
OF TIMOR 6

*

**My name is Major General Peter Cosgrove.
My task is to restore peace and order to East
Timor. I plan to carry out that mission.**

It was at a press conference in Darwin in September
1999 that most Australians laid eyes on Cos for the first
time. Surrounded by a mob of more than 40 national
and international TV camera crews and other media,
he spoke with calm assurance. He had an air of clear
purpose. He looked like a man whose time had come
and he was relishing it.

Cos' appearance in Darwin was the culmination of a
torrential flow of events that had begun to accelerate to
their inevitable conclusion about eight months earlier. In

January 1999, the then Indonesian President B. J. Habibie unexpectedly agreed to a proposal by Prime Minister John Howard that the people of East Timor should be permitted to vote in a referendum on their autonomy. Howard's suggestion had been for a gradual re-evaluation of Indonesia's control of East Timor. Howard had written:

> I want to emphasise that Australia's support for Indonesia's sovereignty is unchanged. It has been a long-standing Australian position that the interests of Australia, Indonesia and East Timor are best served by East Timor remaining part of Indonesia . . . It might be worth considering a means of addressing the East Timorese desire for an act of self-determination in a manner that avoids an early and final decision on the future status of the province. . . . (This) would allow time to convince the East Timorese of the benefits of autonomy within the Indonesian republic.

Speaking in a Senate Hearing in 1999, John Dauth, the Deputy Secretary of the Department of Foreign Affairs, clarified the thinking behind Howard's letter: '. . . a very important part of our thinking at the time that the Prime Minister despatched his letter was that Indonesia really only had one last chance to keep East Timor as part of Indonesia.'

Habibie stunned the Australians when he agreed to an 'independence' ballot. It has since emerged that the

Indonesians mistakenly believed they had the numbers among the East Timorese people to win the vote. Nevertheless, many observers believed that the reports of orchestrated violence coming from East Timor meant that elements of the Indonesian military were taking no chances.

As early as the first months of 1998 Australian military intelligence had begun to pick up some disturbing 'sigint' (electronic signals intelligence, as distinct from 'humint' or human intelligence – that is, spies) relating to East Timor. The sigint was picked up by the Defence Signals Directorate's extensive network of radio and phone listening stations in north and west Australia which monitor South-East Asia. The intelligence showed a sharp increase in militia activity in East Timor, part of Timor, an island that lay at the eastern end of the Indonesian Archipelago, about 800 kilometres north-west of Darwin, sitting between the South China Sea and the Indian Ocean. East Timor was home to about 750,000 people and another 3 million people lived in West Timor. This island had been largely ignored by the general Australian public and the rest of the world, until now.

The intelligence revealed that pro-Indonesia militia groups in East Timor were trying to counter the growing independence movement there with intimidation and violence. By early 1999, new intercepts confirmed what intelligence sources already believed: that the Indonesian military (the Tentara Nasional Indonesia or TNI) and some elements of their Special

Forces (the feared Kopassus) were active in creating what they wanted the outside world to think were spontaneously growing local militia groups determined to fight against the pro-independence forces in East Timor, thus giving the impression that the people were clearly divided on their future and that any violence was the result of a 'civil war' between the factions. The intelligence also revealed the militia was paying poor villagers to take part in the mob unrest. This was not entirely unexpected information. The previous year, prompted by the increased sigint from the region, three intelligence officers within the ADF had completed an intelligence estimate that had formally warned of the impending problems and the possibility of bloodshed in the event that East Timor sought independence. This report was shelved.

As the crisis simmered towards its boiling point in September 1999, Cos was commander of the 1st Australian Division, the Deployable Joint Force (DJF), headquartered in Brisbane. As soon as the ADF became aware of the intelligence and the changed political circumstances, it began exploring contingency plans, which, it believed, would cover the foreseeable developments. These took the form of theoretical 'war games' or 'tewts' (tactical exercises without troops) – centred on evacuating those who may be caught up in the violence – because neither the ADF generally nor Cos and his DJF specifically had the resources to do more. As it turned out, neither their plans nor the scenarios they examined anticipated the scale of the devastation or the speed with which events unfolded. The result would draw the ADF into the biggest and most intricate peace enforcement operation in which it had ever been involved in Australia's region and turn Cos' into the best-known Australian Army commander since World War II.

While the ADF planned, it also consulted with the TNI, drawing on contacts made through many years of joint exercises and exchange studies. The aim was to show respect for Indonesia's position over East Timor while opening up possible channels for future collaboration in handling the escalating violence.

Meanwhile, the violence steadily worsened and peaked on 6 April 1999 with a massacre in Liquica village, about 20 kilometres east of Timor's capital, Dili, where militia surrounded a church in which villagers were sheltering. They dragged out two priests and teargassed those people inside. When they came staggering out, the militia attacked them. They killed between 25 and 50 and injured many more. This mass murder was followed on 17 April by a militia-instigated attack on the homes and families of leading independence supporters in Dili. At least a dozen, as many as 25, people were murdered.

President Habibie's government signed a United Nations-brokered agreement with the former ruler of East Timor, Portugal, in New York on 5 May 1999, under which it agreed to put a referendum to the East Timorese people proposing autonomy under Indonesian rule. From Habibie's viewpoint, a majority vote for autonomy would solve the East Timor problem once and for all. On the other hand, if the East Timorese rejected the proposal, the agreement provided for the United Nations to take control until the country progressed to independence. The agreement gave responsibility for security for the election to the Indonesians.

On 27 May 1999 Australian Foreign Minister Alexander Downer announced that Australia would establish a consulate in Dili to assist in the conduct of the forthcoming referendum. The ADF's initial plan for security support for the election (which was scheduled originally for 8 August, then postponed to 21 August and finally happened on 30 August) was called Operation Concord and consisted largely of RAAF flights to transport UN volunteers, police and military liaison officers to East Timor to assist with the poll. It linked with Operation Faber, which centred on providing military observers to serve with the UN Mission overseeing the vote. The future Commissioner of the Australian Federal Police, Mick Keelty, then an Assistant Commissioner, played a leading role in the Australian Federal Police's (AFP) involvement in the UN operation. AFP officers joined the United Nation's unarmed civilian policing group (Civpol). It was a bold decision to go in unarmed, as demanded by the Indonesians, and the militia swiftly took advantage of the Civpol officers' non-combatant status and lack of arms by constantly harassing them. Although many of the group returned traumatised, they carried out their task so well that they effectively disrupted the militia's plans to destabilise the election and provided sufficient security that some 98 per cent of the registered voters were able to cast ballots. And, despite the pervading climate of fear and violence, just over 78 per cent of them rejected the Indonesian proposal – 344,580 against; 94,388 for. Convinced they would win the vote, the Indonesians had fatally misjudged the situation and now made desperate efforts to salvage it.

Immediately after the election result was declared, on 3 September, a new and far more intense wave of violence exploded as both pro-Indonesian militia and some TNI soldiers turned on the East Timorese and their possessions. They took control of the streets of Dili and torched government and private buildings, destroyed virtually all services – electricity, phone, water and sewage – and murdered many civilians. If the Indonesians were to lose the province they had ruled for 24 years, they were not going to leave anything of value behind them. As much as a third of the population moved, or was moved, into West Timor or overseas.

Along with people from all around the world, Cos and his team watched chilling news footage showing bands of armed pro-Indonesia militia chasing terrified East Timorese refugees into the UN compound in Dili while Indonesian police and military looked on. (Subsequent leaked intelligence has since revealed that TNI were directing the carnage, as detailed in *Masters of Terror* by Hamish McDonald and Des Ball. This was confirmed by the East Timor Commission for Reception, Truth and Reconciliation's 2500-page report handed to UN Secretary General Kofi Annan and Indonesian President Susilo Bambang Yudhoyono, early in 2006.)

The respected Carter Center, a non-profit international aid organisation established by former US President Jimmy Carter, provided an independent snapshot of the situation at the time.

Once the vote results were announced on Saturday, armed pro-integration militia members have erected roadblocks throughout Dili and [taken] control of the streets of the capital at all hours of the day. Militia members are: terrorizing and murdering unarmed civilians; intimidating, threatening, and attacking international personnel; burning houses; and displacing large numbers of people. Carter Center observers have on numerous occasions witnessed militia members perpetrating acts of violence in full view of heavily armed police and military personnel who either stand by and watch or actively assist the militias.

On Monday afternoon, Sept 6, in Dili, reports were received that thousands of internally displaced persons were being taken from their places of refuge in Dili by police and loaded on trucks headed for West Timor. Over the weekend, militia members attacked and burned the offices of the International Committee of the Red Cross, the residence of Nobel Peace Prize laureate Bishop Carlos Belo, and other places of refuge, forcing thousands of internally displaced people sheltered in those places to flee.

Carter Center observers contacted officials at one Catholic mission in Dili that was sheltering several thousand internally displaced persons. They said armed militia had removed all young men from the compound on Monday evening. Their current whereabouts and condition is unknown. Carter Center observers were attacked by militia at the port of Dili as they attempted to evacuate the Carter Center's local East Timorese staff on Sunday. After being pursued through the city by armed militia and by Indonesian police, the Center's international observers were evacuated to Jakarta with the help of the Australian consulate and the US Embassy. Carter Center local staff are still scattered in Dili and unaccounted for.

Elsewhere in Dili, Indonesian police forced most of the international observers and media to travel at gunpoint to Komoro Airport, where they were evacuated by a shuttle of aircraft. This was the ADF's Operation Spitfire – the evacuation of United Nations and foreign nationals by RAAF Hercules aircraft, each protected by two SAS troops. From 6 September to 14 September, the RAAF and the New Zealand Air Force evacuated 2478 Australian consular officials and East Timorese whose lives were in danger. Usually the evacuees arrived in small convoys with a TNI military escort, but militia roadblocks caused lengthy delays and were feeding tensions. The operation almost faltered when Indonesian officials recognised the Nobel Peace Prize laureate Bishop Carlos Belo among the refugees and refused to allow him to leave. After a tense stand-off between the Australians, interpreters and the senior TNI officers, Bishop Belos was allowed to leave with a single aide. As the aircraft taxied for take-off, the Indonesians changed their minds and blocked the runway with a truck full of soldiers. Ten minutes of hard negotiation later, the Indonesians withdrew the truck and the bishop and 127 other evacuees flew to Darwin and safety.

A small band of journalists refused to leave and sought refuge in the UN compound, which soon swelled to bursting after several thousand terrified locals poured in when they were driven out of the nearby school by gunfire. United Nations Mission in East Timor (UNAMET) was forced to evacuate all its eight regional offices and began to evacuate its international staff from its headquarters. But, knowing their departure would have meant certain death to the 1500 or so refugees they were protecting in their compound, the UN staff refused to leave without them. They won the day and the refugees were taken out to Darwin.

The violence may have appeared random and chaotic but many believed it had a carefully calculated underlying purpose. The Australian Army's former principal analyst for East Timor at the time, Major Clinton Fernandes, later wrote in *Reluctant Saviour*:

For all its visceral, punitive aspects, the main objective of Indonesia's terror campaign was to reverse the result of the ballot. It would have to be discredited as rigged, by suggesting that a majority of East Timorese were voting with their feet in accordance with their true wishes.

The plan was that the violence would have masked the further steps in the Indonesians' strategy: to force out all foreign observers and media; to then turn on the local people and herd them over the border into West Timor; to thus provoke the Timorese Freedom Fighters (the Falintil – the military arm of Fretilin, the Revolutionary Front for an Independent East Timor or *Frente Revolucionária do Timor Leste Independente*) to react with violence; to respond to that threat by sending in the TNI to destroy Falintil; and finally to discredit and nullify the ballot by whatever means necessary.

But subsequent events would conspire to negate these plans. It was not until 7 September that the Australian government began to give serious thought to intervening in the situation with an international force and only then did ADF Headquarters establish an East Timor Policy Unit to liaise between the Defence Minister and the ADF executive. The following day, the ADF began formal planning for Operation Warden, our involvement with an international peacekeeping force in East Timor.

The Australian Government's initial efforts to drum up support for the international force met with lukewarm responses, with only Canada, New Zealand, the United Kingdom, Malaysia and Thailand responding positively. This was hardly surprising considering that the Australian Government had previously been vehemently against such an intervention.

★ ★ ★

On 9 September, after considerable prompting from Prime Minister Howard, US President Bill Clinton threatened to withdraw financial aid from Indonesia unless it acted to end the violence. He followed up by cutting US military ties with Indonesia. During a stopover in Hawaii, President Clinton upped the ante by displaying his understanding of the intricacies of the situation: 'It is clear the Indonesian military is aiding and abetting the militia violence . . . This is simply unacceptable.'

Further international pressure followed when the International Monetary Fund (IMF) suspended its Indonesian lending program. Some sources claim Clinton gave the Indonesians a simple choice to 'lose Timor, or lose East Timor'. In other words, lose all of it, or lose half of it: you make the call.

The UN Security Council acted swiftly. On 11 September, President Clinton was supported by the UN General Assembly in calling on Indonesia to invite an international force to restore peace and order in East Timor. The following day President Habibie agreed, and on 14 September the UN Security Council passed a resolution (Resolution 1264 (1999)) calling for the creation of an International Force in East Timor (INTERFET), under Chapter VII of the UN Charter, to intervene in East Timor. The Australian Government offered to lead the force and this was accepted. Cos was appointed to command INTERFET.

From the start, INTERFET had clear aims: to restore peace and security in East Timor; to protect and support UNAMET in carrying out its tasks; and to facilitate humanitarian assistance operations. And, for the first time for a peacekeeping or peacemaking force, the resolution authorised INTERFET 'to take all necessary measures to fulfil this mandate'.

As soon as news of his appointment was made public, Cos received encouraging support from the public and from his peers. Recently retired General John Sanderson told ABC Radio on 15 September 1999:

Oh, he's a soldier's soldier. A very straight shooter. He did a wonderful job at the Royal Military College. Very good with young soldiers. He's got a very strong background in this sort of activity. He was an instructor at the British Staff College earlier in his career, and he would have instructed in the sort of activities that we are talking about in East Timor . . . the obstacle is to get everybody to have confidence in the command structure and to understand what the objectives are and to share those and to cut out the confusion on that and to recognise the fact that, you know, a lot of nations will have a very direct engagement with the activity. So, you know, he may be an operational level commander, but he also engages at the strategic level. That requires a great deal of sensitivity.

Cos was well aware of the need for diplomacy and sensitivity, especially as INTERFET was a combination of troops from 22 countries, from six continents. It was a task for which he'd been preparing for his whole career but one that would test virtually every skill in his kitbag: personal leadership; operational command; strategic thinking and command; multinational cooperation, especially in border and personnel protection; peacekeeping; diplomacy; humanitarian aid; and even nation building.

Just five days after the Security Council's mandate, Australia had coordinated the arrival of the first coalition forces in Dili. By the end of that first day, 19 September, approximately 2300 troops had deployed to East Timor. That they achieved this reflects great credit on Cos and his subordinates. It's only recently that the true levels of lack of preparation with which the force was hamstrung have been revealed. The original ADF plans had focused on Australian troops assisting in the evacuation of foreigners and East Timorese in peril. There had been no plans for Australian troops to spend any extended time on East Timor soil. Consequently, no plans had been made to provide fresh food and water to a long-term deployment force. They had to borrow 4000 flak jackets from the US forces and to scrounge other gear from other units. There was no 'doctrine' (or operational template) developed for regional multinational operations, nor were there sufficient language experts for East Timor.

Despite these handicaps, Cos and his diggers left

Australia with high hopes and warm wishes, as Cos later recalled:

> I've never seen such an outpouring of concern, sympathy, empathy, identification as we experienced when we headed off into Timor. We were heading off into the unknown and in those first few weeks I believe you could have cut the emotional outpouring with a knife that was pouring in through letters, radio broadcasts, television, the whole nine yards. The force was overwhelmed with these messages of concern which uplifted them greatly.
>
> And that was from people who were sort of playing their vicarious role as a digger. A lot of mums and dads and brothers and sisters but, also, a lot of people who simply wanted to identify with the team – being sort of 'Team Australia' but also 'Team Australia in East Timor'.

When Cos landed at Dili's domestic airport, Komoro Field, he and his team were greeted by an ominous haze over Dili: smoke slowly rising from the wholesale devastation wrought by the militia and TNI soldiers. Eight out of every ten buildings were razed to the ground and those still standing bore the scars of the havoc. Power stations, phone lines, water supplies, sewer pipes, drains and all manner of infrastructure were wantonly damaged. The human toll was immediately evident too. The foul smell of ageing faeces mixed with an overwhelming stench of decay warned of even more horrifying discoveries. (Within days of INTERFET's arrival there was evidence of mass murder.) In the initial days, Cos based his advance force at the airport as he set about securing it and the areas surrounding it. The 200-strong US communications forces attached to INTERFET established a satellite and web-based intelligence communications system, which allowed the Australian, British, Canadian and American elements of the force to post intelligence reports on a secret and secure home page on the Hawaiian-based United States Pacific Command server.

As he had done so often in the past, Cos won over his team by leading by example from the start. When he realised there weren't enough flak jackets for everyone he said he wouldn't have one until the last of his soldiers were equipped with them. When he set up his head-quarters in what was left of the Dili Library, a colonial-style three-storey pile, he slept on a stretcher in his office, a charred anteroom just off the operations room. Like almost all the major buildings in the city, it had been torched by the rampaging militia after the referendum but had been sufficiently resurrected to serve its new purpose. The bottom floor housed the military police, the second was home to the air force and navy, and the top floor was a restricted-access area containing the INTERFET headquarters' operations and intelligence cells and Cos' room.

Cos later likened the INTERFET arrival to a 'pool of water' where the forces poured into Dili and spread from there.

When we got here we had to seize the capital city of Dili and branch out from there. And what we needed to do was to patrol the streets and to make sure that violent armed people weren't allowed to roam the streets picking on innocent civilians – men, women and children – and hurting them. Easy to say, but difficult to do because you had to first pick out who were the adversaries and who were the innocents, but the soldiers proved to be very good at that and very quickly the militias, that's what we call the adversary, learned that it was pointless to continue to try to perform their bullying acts and either laid down their weapons or left East Timor.

Cos made an early conscious decision to make positive use of the substantial media contingent observing him and his troops. It reflected his confidence in his communication skills and in the abilities of his men. He looked back on the decision and its benefits in an address after he became Chief of the Defence Force.

I thought it best not just to accept or acquiesce in the media presence in East Timor but to embrace it and encourage it, not just from participant countries' media but from anywhere. I emphasised that we would be transparent, accountable, available and very proactive.

Rather than engage in adversarial rhetoric in relation to some of the grotesque distortions of the truth that characterised a lot of the opposing campaign, I preferred to invite such scrutiny of our broad demeanour and behaviour and the outcomes of our operations to allow people to assess the lies for what they were. I cannot stress enough this aspect of information operations in its crucial contribution to a successful coalition mission. In this area of nurturing your constituencies, you can be figuratively just as damaged by a headline as a bullet.

I have learned over time not to be intimidated by the media, but rather to regard them simply as a medium which will allow me to present simple and clear messages, preferably without evasive or confusing 'officialese', to ordinary and decent Australians. This was the 'mum and dad' test I used when carefully considering and crafting what key messages I wanted to send to the parents and families of our troops on this operation.

But establishing and maintaining public communication channels was only a small part of Cos' initial challenge. He first drew on his leadership to establish his force's credibility, both on the ground and internationally. This was no mean feat when you looked at the state of play and the perilous confusion that greeted him. Cos arrived at the head of about 5000 troops. Indonesia still had 15,000 troops in East Timor. These same troops had, for whatever reason, either participated in or stood by as pro-Indonesian militia destroyed the country's infrastructure and killed many of its inhabitants. Despite the political games being played elsewhere, Cos and his troops faced the very real prospect that a single incident could at any time spark a largely uncontrollable conflict. Respected military historian Professor David Horner notes:

> If it had not been managed properly there could have been the possibility of fighting between Australian and Indonesian troops. Much credit must go to General Cosgrove for his adaptable leadership.
>
> Now we know that before he went on his reconnaissance trip to Dili, he had a plan that the SAS would come in the helicopters to start the landing. But when he went on the reconnaissance he sussed out that this might not be such a good thing, because it would get the Indonesians off-side. We had the agreement of the Indonesians that he could arrive in a Hercules and he would be protected by Indonesian soldiers and that things ought to be put in place so that the landing could be done in a secure way. So he immediately changed the plan. The SAS didn't go in first.
>
> He did it because he wanted to make sure that he could decrease the chances of any conflict involving Australians and he tried to manage things to reduce that possibility of conflict and he was successful in this regard.
>
> It was a bit of a calculated gamble but he had

to resist that idea that we would go in, in such a way that that would be too aggressive but, on the other hand, we did still go in with full combat capability.

And perhaps just as well because had Cos and his force shown signs of weakness the situation could have swiftly degenerated into chaos. While dealing with an ever-changing swell of internal politics within INTERFET as nations manoeuvred to best suit their particular interests, Cos kept his eye on the bigger picture.

At one stage there was a border incident where a number of Indonesian policemen were shooting with automatic weapons, at our soldiers. Another Australian soldier in a slightly different position to the ones who were being shot at could see these men shooting at his mates and did the right thing – shot one of the policemen, killed him. There was no rejoicing over that. It was a matter of regret, of necessity, but of regret.

It was one of many early teething problems associated with the nebulous nature of the border between East and West Timor. The INTERFET patrol had come to a bridge. They had seen what they regarded as clearly identifiable border markers showing that they were still in East Timor. On the other side of the bridge, an outpost, manned by TNI soldiers, officers and Indonesians, was monitoring their movements. When two diggers had tried to cross the bridge with a larger formation behind them, troops from the outpost fired on them. The diggers returned fire.

In the operations room in Dili there was initial confusion about the situation and it threatened to blow up into an international incident when an English-speaking Indonesian liaison officer confronted the operations staff officers, demanding explanations about why his troops had been hit. He'd been in full cry for some minutes when Cos burst out of his office and set the interloper on his heels by poking him in the chest and telling him, 'You'll get your investigation when I get the names of the Indonesian soldiers who fired on my soldiers today. Now get out of my headquarters.'

Cos returned to his office, leaving his staff pumping their fists in appreciation, happy to have a decisive leader who was prepared to stand up for his soldiers. They regarded his actions with even greater admiration because they understood that, although he was still a junior general, he was prepared to make a stand irrespective of the criticism or negative career implications it might have had for him personally. However, Cos, the politically aware communicator, knew the matter had to be handled differently for public consumption.

Part of the public explanation of what had occurred was this: How sad. If that man had not been shooting at our soldiers, he'd be alive today. But you know the message here was: Don't shoot at Australians or that might happen to you. But it could have been put the other way: You shoot at Australian soldiers, you learn your lesson. That wouldn't have gone down well. I guess he's learnt his lesson would have sounded like rejoicing.

I think that people want to be reassured that when their sons and daughters have to apply violence it's a matter of regret, not because they did the wrong thing, but that violence was necessary.

Within the first few days of their arrival, Cos began receiving reports that his troops had discovered evidence of murder and torture. Cos spoke live on ABC TV News on 23 September:

My soldiers are all tremendously professional and I'm very proud of the restraint and the judgement and the discipline they've shown in what's been a very trying first few days. I'm sure, like everybody who is aware of these sorts of findings, they're disgusted, they're horrified, and I know that many Indonesian regular soldiers feel the same way. These horrible excesses are just a sign of how necessary it was that the international community did what it has now done, which is to provide an international force in here to stop the violence.

Within the first week of INTERFET operations, Cos also showed his determination and decisiveness to his superiors back in Canberra. Each evening he would

Cos' grandfather, Jack Cosgrove (far right), in a still from the early Australian movie *Silks and Saddles*, 1921

Cos' father, John (left), and his Uncle Bill, as boys in Melbourne

Cos' father, Captain John Cosgrove, with his wife, Ellen, at an army function, December 1975

Cos (seated on the far right of the front row) in the Waverley College leaving class of 1964

Cos (fourth from the left of the back row) in the Third XV rugby team at RMC Duntroon, 1966

Cos (right) sharing a beer with Duntroon classmates Mike McDermott and Bill Rolfe

Cos hams it up with Mike McDermott and a friend at a Duntroon fancy-dress ball.

Mike McDermott celebrates with Cos at their graduation from RMC Duntroon, 1968

Cos in 9RAR's base camp at Nui Dat in Vietnam, with
a fourteen-foot python, 1970

Nui Dat from the air

9RAR diggers plan an attack, Vietnam, 1969

A 9RAR digger guards a Vietcong bunker
entrance

The late Lieutenant Bob Convery, Vietnam, 1969

Cos' company commander, Captain Graham Dugdale

Diggers from 9RAR head out on patrol, Vietnam, 1969

The 9RAR sergeants' mess bar at Nui Dat

Cos (second from the right, leaning down) in B Company, 9RAR's rugby team, Nui Dat, 1969

9RAR heads home from Vung Tau Harbour, Saigon

write a succinct situation report for secret transmission back to Operations Headquarters in the bunker below the ADF's Russell Offices. Usually it ran to 300 or 400 words. One evening it was much briefer.

That day, two diggers were wounded in an ambush while they were transporting captured militia back over the West Timor border. The convoy they were travelling in was led into the ambush by TNI troops. The leading truck was seen to weave over the road as a signal. One of the diggers was shot in the neck and the other in the leg. Cos was furious. It was a serious breakdown in trust with very dangerous implications. That evening, instead of writing a detailed summary of the incident, Cos wrote just four words. 'The gloves are off!'

The following day Cos placed an infantry battalion as a blocking force at one end of Dili and mounted another battalion in armoured personnel carriers at the other end. INTERFET had identified a number of known militia haunts, not difficult because they were in some of the very few buildings not burned to the ground. Cos ordered his mobile force to sweep through the city and clean out the militia elements in a day. It was a clear message of intent. The captured militia soldiers were questioned. Those not posing a direct threat were released, in accordance with INTERFET's rules of engagement, which required that those released be offered the choice of escort to Indonesian authorities. None accepted the offer, nor were they compelled to do so.

Despite the confrontations, Cos has consistently credited the benefits of the network of personal relationships that had been established between the Australian military and those from other regional nations, as helping to avoid the sparks that could have ignited a conflagration. Cos knew his INTERFET deputy, General Songkitti from Thailand, from his stint at the British Army Staff College at Camberley in the mid-1980s. He knew the commander of the US forces assigned to help with INTERFET's communications, Brigadier John Castellaw, as well as many of the commanders of the other participating nations, and their superiors at home.

Each of the regional contributors to the force was assigned an Australian liaison officer who spoke their language, knew their culture and had developed personal relationships with them, often fostered during exchange training.

Cos also put great energy into gaining the trust and support of the local East Timorese people. He was an impressive figurehead for the changed state of affairs as he moved about Dili, making personal contact with locals and winning their confidence. His aim was to achieve a balance between the threat of force his troops represented and the desire to end the violence peacefully. In doing so, Cos was well aware of the convoluted history that had brought East Timor to its present crossroads.

★ ★ ★

Six decades earlier, during World War II, the diggers of Sparrow Force fought an extraordinary guerrilla campaign against an overwhelmingly superior Japanese invasion force that planned to use Timor as a base. (Interestingly, this was technically a breach of Portugal's sovereignty and neutrality.) Some of the local people fought with Sparrow Force, while many others gave them supplies and warned them of Japanese approaches. These people paid a terrible price for their collaboration. Historians believe up to 60,000 East Timorese were killed by the Japanese during the occupation. In 1953, the Portuguese bloodily suppressed a Timorese uprising. In 1975, the island was invaded by Indonesia. From then until INTERFET's intervention, between 100,000 and 180,000 East Timorese people perished from starvation, disease and as casualties from the occupying forces. The East Timor Commission for Reception, Truth and Reconciliation reported in 2006 that Jakarta had made a conscious decision to use starvation against the civilian population in East Timor and it resulted in these deaths out of a population of 650,000. The report also found Indonesia guilty of violations of the Third and Fourth Geneva Conventions and the regulations annexed to the Fourth Hague Convention, many amounting to crimes against humanity and war crimes.

Cos knew how shabbily Australia had treated East Timor since the days of Sparrow Force. When Indonesia invaded it in December 1975 and annexed it on 16 July 1976, only three nations officially recognised the annexation: Australia, India and Papua New Guinea, although the United States gave it tacit compliance.

A secret cable from Australia's Ambassador to Indonesia, Richard Woolcott, to the Head of the Foreign Affairs

Department in Canberra perfectly exemplified the Australian approach.

> Policies should be based on disengaging ourselves as far as possible from the Timor situation. We should leave events to take their course; and if and when Indonesia does intervene, act in a way which would be designed to minimise the public impact in Australia and show privately understanding to Indonesia of their problems ... I know I am recommending a pragmatic rather than a principled stand, but that is what national interest and foreign policy is all about.

The United Nations passed a grand-sounding but hollow resolution condemning Indonesia's invasion but took no action. Resolution 3485 read, 'Recognising the inalienable right of all peoples to self-determination ... Calls upon all States to respect the inalienable right of the people of Portuguese Timor to self-determination.'

The reality was that Australia, the United States and her allies chose the maintenance of relations with Indonesia, the world's biggest Muslim country, as a trading partner and ally over the rights of the people of a tiny island. The prevailing view – one upheld by a succession of Australian governments of both political persuasions over the period – was that a united Indonesia, even under a dictator, was preferable to the likely alternative, which was assessed as being its chaotic fragmentation into a warring rabble of tiny independent states. In fact, Indonesia's invasion and its brutal occupation and violent suppression of the remarkably resilient East Timor resistance movement largely escaped international condemnation. Only in the early 1990s, after graphic video footage of the Dili massacre was smuggled out, did Indonesia's human rights abuses finally attract international attention, largely due to the work of two East Timorese activists, Bishop Carlos Filipe Ximenes Belo and José Ramos Horta, who shared the 1996 Nobel Peace Prize for their work.

As Cos found during his time in East Timor, there were still people alive who vividly remembered the Australian presence in World War II. As a combat veteran, that was something that sustained him during some of his worst times, as did his pride in the performance of his diggers, especially in their compassion.

I think we carry our national characteristics with us, we don't subordinate any important element of the Australian character in the making and the life of a digger. For example, we still very much have a sense of social justice, which applies not just internally to the army but in our dealings with other people. So I would be amazed if Australian soldiers seeing people of other nations suffering hardship, which they do if they go to an area of operations they will see people who are down and out, if this doesn't strike a tremendous chord in the digger's heart.

I can recall in the Oecussi enclave a young

corporal from Support Company 3RAR. These troops were our security force down there and I was visiting them. I used to visit them on frequent occasions. I was way down in one end of the Oecussi enclave about as remote as you can get and in amongst a group of about 10 or 15 3RAR soldiers when this corporal said, 'Sir, can we get a doctor down here?' And I said, 'Why, are you crook?'

He said, 'No, we're all right and we see our doctor or the medico from time to time when we need them, but where I am I'm down right on this little village and there's just us infantry soldiers here and we need a doctor for the locals.'

I said, 'Yeah, well, I suppose I could look into that but you know we're still struggling to get the medical system laid out here in all of East Timor. What's the story?'

He answered, 'Well, about a week ago a bloke brought his wife to me and she was having a baby and he was tearing his hair out because she was in very strong labour and he didn't know what to do and we just got on with it.'

I said, 'What do you mean?'

He said, 'Well, we delivered the baby.'

I said, 'Was that a first for you?'

He said, 'Absolutely. In the end it was reasonably uncomplicated, everything worked out okay and baby's all right, the mother's made a good recovery and that's fine.'

I said, 'Oh, good. All's well that ends well.'

And he said, 'Yeah, but yesterday a lady presented with a breech birth . . . I'm not real good on those!'

By the end of October Cos was publicly calling on the UN to provide special investigators into the atrocities his troops were uncovering.

From our point of view, we couldn't go any harder. I'd like to see more expert investigative capability on the ground. I think that'd be great . . . I don't know what the issues have been. All I know is I can use them. I could have used them last week, and I can certainly use them this week. So the sooner they get here the better.

Cos was careful to avoid openly either accusing the Indonesians of involvement in the atrocities or apportioning blame for the various border incidents in which INTERFET soldiers had been involved. The underlying aim for his diplomacy was to maximise the chances of cooperation to ensure the safe return of as many refugees from West Timor as possible as he confirmed on ABC TV News on 30 October:

There are so many different and complex emotions at play. If we are resolute but sensitive in our treatment of this issue, in the end the people who really count, who are the IDPs (the displaced people), will get back safe and sound.

By the end of November, INTERFET had secured the situation sufficiently for Prime Minister John Howard to spend about three hours touring the area. He spoke on his return to Darwin of the 'terrific job' that INTERFET had done.

> I wanted to thank as many of them as I could in the time available. They are great Australians who've done a tremendous job for our country and in the process, with General Cosgrove's leadership, brought enormous repute to Australia around the world . . . It's a scene of immense desolation, and it's very obvious when you fly over the towns in a helicopter that some areas have been systematically burnt and destroyed, and other areas have been completely spared. The areas that have been torched are just still in ruins, and a lot of work will be required to rebuild them. But the good news is that the people are coming back. They are recovering their spirit. They see in the INTERFET forces, particularly in our own, because we're the most numerous, people who are their friends and their protectors . . .
>
> General Cosgrove told me that if you looked at that part of his mandate of restoring peace and stability, that that had been substantially achieved. And certainly the security position on the ground in East Timor is dramatically better and different and more safe than it was when the troops first went there on 20 September.

While INTERFET forces were making great progress in pacifying large areas of East Timor, the East–West Timor border continued as a possible flashpoint, with many instances of militia and TNI forces firing on INTERFET troops across the border. Cos was forced to chopper in additional troops and on 20 December he wrote to his Indonesian military counterparts expressing his concern at the possible consequences if the clashes continued.

On that same day a bizarre event was noticed by INTERFET's intelligence cell in Dili. Someone back in Australia pulled the plug allowing the INTERFET computers access to their top-secret Australian database, known as TOPIC. For more than 24 hours that access was denied, at a time when Australian and multinational troops were in harm's way and relying on the flow of intelligence. This extraordinary and unprecedented action has never been satisfactorily explained. It would haunt the Australian intelligence community for years and send shocks through the upper echelons of the organisation.

For Cos, it was just one of the myriad problems that he and his team had to solve on the run by the hour and by the day. He drummed into all his subordinates one of the greatest lessons he learned from his time in Vietnam – never relax for an instant. He knew how the grind of continuous patrolling could lull troops into a sense of secure familiarity and how that can be the instant when fate strikes. He tried to set an example through his own behaviour and his attention to detail that would encourage them to treat every day as though it could be the one where their luck ran out, and to maintain their vigilance despite the open-ended nature of their commitment.

Personally, it was an exhausting period for Cos. Because of the need for constant communication with his superiors in Australia, he survived on little sleep and even during the meagre hours when he managed to close his eyes, his mind raced with the doubts experienced by every commander of a great military enterprise: second-guessing decisions; a gnawing concern for the welfare of those you've sent into danger; and the regret for individual tragedies, like the loss of a lance corporal who succumbed to complications from dengue fever in the force's hospital.

Cos was leading INTERFET in the glare of the world media, while being supported unseen by one of his most able colleagues back in the 'pit', the ADF Command Centre's (ADFCC) bunker in the bowels of the Russell Offices in Canberra. The ADFCC was run by Cos' old friend General Michael Keating who, as Assistant Chief of the Defence Force Operations, oversaw the ADF's operations and plans and linked with other divisions within the ADF – strategic, international, policies, development, and so on.

In the normal course of events, Cos would have reported to the theatre commander in Sydney but because of the strategic importance of the international coalition, Cos reported to the Chief of the Defence Force, Admiral Chris Barrie, via Michael Keating. It was Barrie who put those arrangements in place, on Keating's advice. The chain of command continued from the CDF to the Minister for Defence, John Moore.

It was also Michael Keating who helped draft the rules of engagement for Cos' force, drawing on information from around the world, managing the convoluted coalitions involved and integrating them into future joint plans.

Colleagues still speak with admiration of Keating's dedication as he spent long hours in the bunker every day for months during the crisis. Each morning, Cos' most important 5 am phone call was to Keating, who kept him across the ever-changing issues affecting him: strategic issues in Canberra; internal politics within the military; politics in general; the state of the nation with each of the members of the coalition; details of any atrocities coming forward through his sources; etcetera.

Cos has always praised Keating's enormous capacity for work and his ability to organise his staff to shape the way the venture was progressing while, at the same time, being able to guard Cos' back. Keating provided invaluable 'top cover' for Cos whenever any of the participating nations tried to play him off a break by dealing through other channels to achieve their aims. Keating's input enabled them to speak with one voice. Few of their colleagues missed the irony that two of the biggest competitors for the position of Chief of the Army (with General Peter Abigail) were inextricably linked. It was a measure of the character and leadership of Michael Keating, and his ideals of loyalty and service, that he selflessly carried out his role. (Cos tried to repay the loyalty a few years down the track when Keating was given early retirement by providing an appropriate farewell from the service but Keating declined the offer.)

Cos worked closely with the head of UNAMET, Brazilian diplomat Sergio Viera de Mello, a 30-year UN veteran who had worked with great effect in many of the world's trouble spots and would play a critical role in East Timor's transition to nationhood. It was de Mello who oversaw the work of peacekeepers and the distribution of humanitarian aid and presided over the establishment of the new nation's judiciary, police, public service and parliament. He and Cos forged a close friendship and working relationship. Cos was deeply saddened when de Mello was killed by a car bomb in Baghdad in August 2003.

Cos also met and worked with another charismatic leader, José Ramos Horta, recognised as the father of the new nation. For a quarter of a century, he kept the flames of East Timor's nationhood alive by working assiduously at the United Nations and by lobbying continuously at the Foreign Affairs departments of nations around the globe. Cos respected Horta's passion and his leadership skills, particularly in the way he was able to hold together his countrymen during the difficult transition period after the independence referendum.

Gradually, INTERFET's presence and the world scrutiny it received saw the Indonesians reduce their military presence in East Timor. By November 1999, the Indonesian force dropped from around 20,000 troops to about 1500.

★ ★ ★

By mid-February 2000 Cos and his force, including 7000 Australians, had been in East Timor for five months and they were counting down the days to their return home. Interviewed on ABC TV News shortly before he completed the mission, he could only point to one regret – the refugees still in West Timor:

> They're outside our mandate. We actually can't do much more than we've done to help secure their release. But I do regret the fact that there are so many of them still in camps unsure of the situation here in East Timor because they've been denied that information or feeling intimidated about making their return. That's really an issue of great regret. There's not a lot I can do about it, but I still regret that I didn't see them return while I was here.

By all accounts, Cos' mission to restore 'peace and security' to East Timor had been a resounding success. As he prepared to withdraw his troops, their mission completed, Cos received accolades from Sergio de Mello and from East Timor's leaders Xanana Gusmao and José Ramos Horta.

At a farewell ceremony in Dili on 23 February 2000 Xanana Gusmao read a passage written by one of Sparrow Force's diggers: 'Money cannot repay the East Timorese for their loyalty in saving the lives of Australian soldiers.'

Xanana Gusmao then addressed Cos.

> General, you have now paid the debt and the East
> Timorese people honour you for that. We thank
> you personally and we thank all INTERFET
> from our hearts. When the children of our nation
> learn of the sacrifices made by all of our martyrs,
> they will learn also of the role of INTERFET.

Cos was obviously moved and he replied, 'We're absolutely delighted with the signs of affection and regard
that have been given to us by the East Timorese leadership and the people.'

After the farewell, the sentiments remained for Cos:

> It was an emotional moment for me and probably
> quite a few of my military colleagues to see that a
> military force can come into a country for five
> months and walk away with the people cheering it.

Military historian Professor David Horner put the
mission into perspective.

> We need to look at East Timor in the broad sweep
> of Australian history. It wasn't fighting – the battle
> was largely avoided. But that is a bit of an unfair
> comparison because it was a very tricky opera-
> tion. Potentially it could have turned nasty and it
> was a coalition operation, a joint operation
> involving the deployment of a large force offshore

from Australia, so there's a geographic logistic environment. Therefore it really was a very big challenge for any commander.

General Cosgrove did exceptionally well. He assessed very quickly that the PR side was very important. Every day he said that he was talking to the mums and dads back home. The winning of the media battle was very important and again, commanders in the past haven't worried about that.

He understood the environment in which commanders have to operate. He'd had major command appointments, so he understood all this. And yes, it could have gone badly but I think that he did very, very well.

Other observers make the point that while INTERFET was sent to East Timor because of the massive national and international protests prompted by Indonesia's actions there, rather than because of the Howard Government's goodwill, it achieved outstanding positive results. They point out that had INTERFET taken even a week or so longer to arrive, more than half of the East Timorese population would have been transported over the West Timor border and the country's leadership and human skill base would have been decimated. In this light, and with his initial preparation constraints, Cos' achievements are all the more praiseworthy.

With the benefit of hindsight, Cos pinpointed a number of crucial areas that underpinned INTERFET's success, including: moulding the coalition forces into a team that felt it was engaged in a 'large and noble venture'; and the careful creation of the participating international 'team' so that each member saw themselves and was seen by the others as equal partners. He would later confirm this when speaking as CDF.

> Arguably forging and maintaining this Alliance was the most difficult thing we undertook in East Timor. But it was vitally essential as all that was good and constructive flowed from it.
>
> Being a leader also takes consistency and moral courage. The word consistency here is important. The volatility of the East Timor situation required that I employ a consistent approach, across the board, to very diverse interest groups: to members of the INTERFET coalition or Alliance; to the East Timorese people themselves; to TNI and militia elements; to the international media; and to the component parts of UNTAET who took over from us, once the security situation had been stabilised at the end of February 2000.

Major General Peter Cosgrove by Tom Alberts, 2001

East Timorese separatist leader Xanana Gusmao chats with Nobel Laureate José Ramos Horta during a press conference at Gusmao's detention house in Jakarta, July 1999

Cos shares a laugh with East Timor's Nobel Peace Laureate Bishop Carlos Belo during a visit to his residence in Dili, October 1999

Cos with members of the multinational peace monitoring forces at their evening meal, East Timor, 2000

Brazilian diplomat Sergio de Mello and Cos, having signed over control from INTERFET to UNTAET, February 2000

Cos is reunited with his wife, Lynne, in Sydney after five months in East Timor, February 2000

Cos leads INTERFET troops as they're welcomed home and presented the keys to the city of Sydney, April 2000

Cos is presented with the Order of Australia by the Queen at Government House in Canberra, March 2000

Cos receives a convoy briefing by Commander Lieutenant Ben Kelly in Iraq, November 2003

As Chief of the Defence Force Cos attends the Iraqi Coastal Defence Force (ICDF) graduation ceremony at Umm Qasr, September 2004

Cos meets members of the ICDF at Umm Qasr, September 2004

Cos talking to troops at the Regional Assistance Mission, Solomon Islands (RAMSI), essentially a Federal Police mission on the islands, August 2003

As the outgoing Chief of the Defence Force, Cos says goodbye to staff at the Defence Headquarters in Canberra, July 2005. His wife, Lynne, and the new Air Chief Marshal, Angus Houston, stand behind him

Mick Keelty, the Commissioner for the Australian Federal Police, at his headquarters in Canberra

As leader of Cyclone Larry Operation Recovery, Cos visits emergency relief workers on the Atherton Tablelands, March 2006

Surveying the damage in the town of Silkwood, near Innisfail, after
being appointed to lead the reconstruction effort, March 2006

THE
CHIEF
7

By the time he arrived back in Sydney after spending 157 hectic days in East Timor, Cos had become, in the words of *The Age*, 'the army's human face'. Millions of Australians, accustomed to a steady but unsatisfying diet of prefabricated plastic celebrities, recognised him as an authentic character and took him to their hearts.

Cos stood out in full technicolour against Australia's dull grey political backdrop. In a world of weasel words, he was a breath of fresh air. Unassuming yet assured, powerful yet non-threatening, he impressed with his clear speaking, his sense of occasion and his undoubted stage presence. That old stager Grandpa Jack Cosgrove would have been proud of him.

When the Minister for Defence, John Moore, officially welcomed him home in Sydney on 24 February 2000

Cos was one of the most popular and best-known people in the country. Moore showered him with praise:

> Peter Cosgrove has earned the respect and gratitude of all Australians for the compassionate and courageous way he conducted our nation's contribution to the United Nations mission in East Timor.
>
> He led by fine example, commanding the largest, most complex military operation undertaken by Australia since the Vietnam War. It was an operation that saw thousands of Australian men and women go into harm's way, with not one life lost under fire. By any measure, this has been an extraordinarily successful outcome.

For Cos it was an especially proud day because Lynne and his three boys were at the airport to greet him. While Cos had been in Dili, his middle son, Philip, had joined the Army Reserves, completed his recruit training and then transferred to the regular army. Cos was touched that the khaki tradition had extended to another generation. As he listened to the speeches of welcome, Cos was also well aware that his career had taken a sharp upturn. He had left for Timor believing it was likely to be his last major posting. Now he was powering past his rivals.

A few weeks before he came home, Cos had called Lynne with the news that he'd been given the nod to become the army's Land Commander, based at Sydney's

Victoria Barracks. They were delighted because it was a major appointment. Of course, it meant yet another move for the family. Lynne had just supervised the move to their new Sydney home, when, just three days before Cos' scheduled return from Timor, he called saying they might have to move again. The word was that he looked like being made Chief of the Army, which would mean moving back to Canberra.

This was a seismic career shift. When he'd been appointed commander of 1 Division, Cos would have expected two years in the job. It was a junior general's job and nobody jumped from there to Chief of the Army. His next-best bet would have been Commander of the Australian Theatre or Head of Training Command. After two years in these posts he might then have been in line for Chief of the Army.

But after Timor, Cos moved ahead in leaps and bounds. He had arrived back physically and mentally exhausted but he had little time to rest and reflect. Back home in late February 2000 as Land Commander, within five months he was named Chief of the Army, jumping over his old rivals: Peter Abigail, who had been in Canberra as Deputy Chief of the Army; and Michael Keating, who had already served as Head of Training Command prior to running the East Timor operation from the Russell Offices bunker as head of Strategic Command. Peter Abigail moved to Land Commander, taking over from Cos, and Peter Leahy, who had been Chief of Staff, Theatre, during East Timor, jumped up to Deputy Chief of the Army.

These were political decisions. The Cabinet, acting on advice from the Defence Minister, has the final say on appointments like the Chief of each of the services or the Chief of the Defence Force (CDF). The minister may take advice from his Department Secretary, the current Chief of the service and/or the CDF but the final decision is a political one. If the minister has no strong views of his own, the other views may carry great weight but if he has a strong view then they can please themselves. Clearly, Cos' outstanding performance in East Timor and his impeccable public standing carried irresistible weight at the political level.

★ ★ ★

For Lynne, the hassle of yet another move was mollified by the beautiful residence in Duntroon into which they moved in July 2000. For Cos, his return to the familiar Duntroon surroundings for the second time in a couple of years added to his comfort level as he eased into the role he had long cherished but never realistically believed he would attain.

Cos had only just settled into his role as Chief of the Army when, in January 2001, he was named Australian of the Year. It was perhaps the clearest illustration of the impact that he had made on the Australian psyche. The official announcement said, 'If there is one word that sums up a sense of duty and courage for Australians, it is ANZAC . . . and if there is one man, who in modern times, embodies the legacy of the ANZAC spirit, it is Lieutenant General Peter Cosgrove.'

The appointment meant even greater public attention and led to a tidal wave of invitations to events, great and small, across the country. His mates delighted in taunting him that 'he'd go to the opening of an envelope', but to Cos it was both a duty and a pleasure and he won many hearts and minds with the warmth of his presence and his simple heartfelt messages. He also learned immensely from the many inspirational Australians he met.

Not surprisingly, Cos' rapidly growing public profile gave rise to criticism, from within and outside the military. Some of this had its genesis in petty jealousy. Some were a classic case of the 'tall poppy' syndrome. Others claimed to be seeking to set the record straight. They would point out that while Cos was the undoubted figurehead of the East Timor campaign, the man who, in military terms, 'ran' our involvement in East Timor was the then CDF, Admiral Chris Barrie. As CDF, Cos would later go on to *run* Australia's commitment to Iraq but in East Timor he *led* INTERFET, supported by General Michael Keating and under the strategic control of Admiral Chris Barrie. These critics would also be at pains to point out that there were many other fine commanders who could have been chosen to lead INTERFET, who would have done just as good a job as Cos. This may well be a fair point. However, Cos was chosen and the others weren't. And Cos performed outstandingly in the role, despite being severely hampered by the 'standing start' after the political prevarication. He showed great political and emotional intelligence in managing the desires, demands and needs of the forces and the masters of the 22 nations thrown together in a scene of unpredictable chaos. Cos was given the opportunity, and he grabbed it. Whenever he was given the chance to take a more senior role, he did the same thing. At each level, Cos showed he was both capable and ready.

One of his most moving moments in his new role came in September 2001 when he became the first Chief of the Army to visit Vietnam since the war. He met with his former foe's senior soldiers in Hanoi and the new Saigon, Ho Chi Minh City, and welcomed the new era of peaceful cooperation. The memories flooded back when he met with some veterans from the units with which he had done battle 30 years earlier. Like veterans down through the years, their shared experiences brought a mutual respect that was clearly evident despite the language barrier. The highlight was a visit to the battlefield at Long Tan, scene of the heroic stand by D Company 6RAR on 18 August 1966 when they held off a massive Vietcong force. Cos had visited the area once during his tour of duty in Vietnam in 1969 but his latest visit made a deep impression. He mentally relived the conflict as he walked the sacred ground and saw the bullet and shrapnel scars on the surviving trees.

Cos returned from Vietnam via Kuala Lumpur. There, Lynne joined him so they could attend the Pacific Armies Chiefs Conference. On the evening of 10 September, they were attending a large reception when a buzz raced around the room. Something about a plane crashing into the World Trade Center in New York. Suspecting the worst, Cos and Lynne returned to their hotel and there, like billions of people around the world, they watched the world change before their eyes.

Cos knew this emergence of terrorism on a global scale would inevitably mean a change in the world order and would surely draw a deadly response from the outraged American victims. He also knew he and his colleagues would be faced with a new and frightening challenge and that, in all likelihood, the role of the armed forces would never be the same again. The next morning, Cos and Lynne joined the exodus from Kuala Lumpur as the conference participants rushed home to plan and execute responses to the new threat.

Back home, Cos was immediately swept up in the Howard Government's response, orchestrated by the CDF, Admiral Chris Barrie. They had decided to support the US-led targeting of Afghanistan as a willing haven for terrorists. For his part, Cos liaised in the provision of a squadron of SAS troops. It was a relatively small force but Australia was stretched because of its continuing commitment in East Timor. The SAS (or the 'chicken stranglers' in digger parlance after their Spartan training exercises which often involved being given live chickens as their only sustenance) were regarded as the most effective small force that the Australian military could contribute to the Afghanistan response. They were our most highly trained troops in counter-terrorism and they had worked extensively with US forces. Within weeks, the SAS were on the ground as part of Operation Slipper in Afghanistan. Cos worked with the commander of the SAS, Brigadier Duncan Lewis, on the preparation of their deployment and on their maintenance once they were in action. He also liaised with Chris Barrie on the Army's contribution to the overall prosecution of the 'War Against Terror'. It would be an excellent apprenticeship for his forthcoming role in Australia's involvement in Iraq.

★ ★ ★

During the lead-up to the 2001 Federal Election Cos received an early warning of the treacherous waters through which he would have to navigate the ADF. The Howard government skilfully exploited what became known as the 'children overboard' affair. The Navy's HMAS *Adelaide* intercepted a 'suspected illegal entry vessel' (or SIEV) off Christmas Island. Designated SIEV 4, the unseaworthy vessel contained asylum seekers and was believed to be operated by people smugglers aiming to deliver them to Australian territory. From 7 October, first the Immigration Minister, Philip Ruddock, then Defence Minister Peter Reith and the Prime Minister claimed that 'a number of children had been thrown overboard' from the vessel when it was detained. They showed photos of children in the water.

These claims were political dynamite, just one month out from the election. The Howard Government was able to use the event to highlight the need for tighter border control while depicting the Labor Opposition as weak and indecisive on the issue. It touched a nerve with voters and the Howard Government was comfortably re-elected.

★ ★ ★

A subsequent Senate inquiry found that not only were the claims untrue and the government knew them to be untrue before the election, but they decided to say nothing. The photos had been taken after the SIEV 4 sank and the asylum seekers were being rescued from the sea.

The episode not only highlighted the way political expediency can take advantage of dubious circumstances, it also revealed some serious communication flaws and confusion in the ADF's chain of command. Chris Barrie found himself mired in the affair's turgid aftermath. His conflicted and indecisive behaviour at the Senate inquiry and in his subsequent recanting of some of the evidence he gave there, prompted *The Australian* to editorialise on 28 February 2002:

> If Admiral Chris Barrie were not retiring in four months as Chief of the Defence Force he would have to be sacked. His humiliating recanting yesterday of Senate testimony delivered only a week ago has cast grave doubt on his ability to command the respect of the men and women who serve under him.
>
> The belated admission that asylum seekers' children were not thrown into the sea has exposed him as someone who exercised poor judgement by refusing on repeated occasions to accept the

word of his officers, or to make his own inquiries to establish the truth. Barrie gave false evidence to ministers and gave false evidence to a parliamentary committee. He acted in a way that was politically useful to a government desperate to win a third term and later to defend its appalling conduct in the children overboard affair. Possibly worst of all, he hung his own officers out to dry by disputing their account of events. In his own words, the reputation of the forces has been damaged.

As the paper conceded, at least Barrie did the honourable thing and owned up in the end. The government didn't, and hasn't. For Cos, it was a timely warning of the minefields ahead.

★ ★ ★

By early 2002 speculation was increasing that Cos was at short odds to be named the new Chief of the Defence Force. His time as Chief of the Army had certainly strengthened his hand and his public profile had increased substantially because of his time as Australian of the Year. Few were surprised when, on 29 May, the Prime Minister called a press conference to announce that Cos would be promoted to General and begin his three-year term as CDF from 4 July 2002. The Prime Minister also advised that Vice-Admiral Russ Shalders would become Cos' deputy and that Peter Leahy, as a Lieutenant General, would replace Cos as Chief of the Army.

Both Cos and the outgoing CDF, Admiral Chris Barrie, were present at the subsequent press conference where journalists' questioning unearthed some interesting exchanges. Chris Barrie alluded to those who might have their noses put out of joint by the appointments.

I know the choices have been tough and I know there will be some disappointed people in the ADF [in] that they weren't able to be selected. Nonetheless, this is a very strong team. It's got a good range of skills and capabilities, very strong leadership profile. And so I look forward to the ADF going on and delivering even better results in the future.

Cos responded:

I'm greatly honoured by my selection of Chief of the Defence Force and very much aware of the great responsibilities imposed upon the Chief. And I'll be working hard to create around me the sense of teamwork and professionalism that is necessary to discharge that office. I'd like to very warmly congratulate and thank the outgoing team on the tremendous results and performance they produced in an extraordinarily busy time for the ADF and make a pledge that we will continue to look after the ADF in the best possible, professional style for all those many thousands of service men and women we're responsible for, and of course for their nearest and dearest, and for the people.

I'd like to say I look forward very much with the team to working for the minister and the government and through the government for the Australian people. And I'd like to congratulate the new team, most warmly. They're a tremendous bunch of people that I happen to know very well indeed. I'm very confident that this leadership team can look after the ADF in the manner that the Australian people will expect. I particularly note that I'll have Air Marshal Angus Houston, a close friend and a very professional colleague and leader, as part of the team.'

The Prime Minister, Barrie and Cos then negotiated their way through queries on the 'children overboard' affair, the subsequent inquiry and the dangers of politicising the military forces. Cos was his usual forthright self.

Be in no doubt the ADF must always work closely with the government because after all, through the government we are serving the people. And I expect that we will work to have a clear and professional and accountable relationship with the government on everything we do. And I expect that is what every other senior leader and subordinate thinks I must do in relation to the government. I will be looking forward to working extraordinarily closely with our elected leaders.

. . . My observation as I travel through the army is that folks in the army are focused on the job. They know that the Australian people rate them very highly and every time the government has expressed its opinion about the ADF they have said that we are performing very satisfactorily and deserve some praise. I'm working on that basis.

At the formal change of command ceremony on 3 July 2002 Cos described Barrie as 'wise, tireless, decisive and strong at a time when his office demanded those qualities'.

Chris Barrie felt the need to point out that in his four years as CDF, he'd served under four Ministers for Defence and six Ministers Assisting and Parliamentary Secretaries, which contributed to a period of 'turbulence and change' in which the ADF was busier than any time since World War II. He also made a point of expressing his regret at the loss of 353 asylum seekers from another SIEV-X but pointed out that no ADF vessels had received any distress calls or knew where the vessel foundered.

★ ★ ★

Cos was well prepared for the challenge as CDF. Few previous incumbents had held more commands as they rose through the ranks. Although his time at the highest level had been relatively short, his wide network of friends and acquaintances in positions of power and influence around the nation and the world gave him an excellent working base. He had developed the ability to take in and distil information, the patience to listen before acting and the instinct to judge character.

But he could still be shaken out of his comfort zone – just as the average Australian was on Saturday, 12 October 2002. Cos and Lynne were enjoying a few days' leave. Both cricket tragics, they had nodded off listening to radio descriptions of the Australians playing Pakistan in Sharjah. Lynne woke in the early hours to the news that a bomb had gone off at the Sari Club in Bali. She roused Cos, who sprang into action, helping to organise the ADF response to the medical assistance and evacuations. Watching the full extent of the horror unfold on television, Cos felt great pride in the way the average Aussies there responded.

> That's the real people, Australians automatically form teams, they bond. We can't see another Australian without feeling an immediate strong sense of identity and you've immediately got a team. I mean in a situation like that, people who wouldn't even have noticed each other in the club but now were seeing each other in the shattered aftermath, turned to each other and took care of each other, forming these immediate lifesaving little teams and that's because we instinctively trust each other until something happens to say the trust was misplaced.
> And that's why Australians are almost as a

fundamental premise so good when they put a military uniform on. You don't have to put a uniform on to have the qualities of a digger, when you do put the uniform on we expect the qualities of a digger and you don't have to dig very deep to find them.

Cos would later reveal that the ADF had no specific plan for the bombings and the difficulty of responding was exacerbated by Bali's relative remoteness, the number and extent of the casualties needing to be evacuated, the continuing terrorist threat and the start of a massive Australian-Indonesian crime investigation. Cos let his instincts take over to a large extent.

> We had some aspects of the requirement covered in a variety of plans, but we were putting it together and sometimes making it up as we went along. In the early hours of the Sunday morning here in Canberra, I woke to hear the first reports of the bombing, which only spoke of explosions and 'some' casualties. I smelt a rat and got action going at Defence Headquarters, which intensified as more information came to hand.
>
> Here is another observation on leadership at times of national adversity: facts and hard information are always going to be better than instinct, but in the absence of the former, in the absence of facts and hard information, be prepared to go with instinct. Even with modern communications

means, our decision making in response to crises such as terrorist attacks must not be ponderous. There are inevitably inbuilt delays to our actions and our decision-making, therefore, must be slick, quick and accurate. Let the leader not be the obstacle.

The Bali tragedy saw the Department of Foreign Affairs, the Australian Federal Police, state police forces and the ADF work together with unprecedented cooperation. The AFP Commissioner, Mick Keelty, rose to the occasion brilliantly and Cos was generous in his praise.

Mick Keelty came into his own as a public figure. He provided enormous leadership, motivation, drive, professionalism, professionally excellent organisational skill to mobilise his own police force and get them moving up there to relieve the very great concerns Australians had that this incident should be prosecuted, in company with Indonesia, to the most rigorous degree.

Cos saw the ADF's role as complementary to that of the other organisations involved – primarily providing medical evacuation and on-the-ground help. Its first and most difficult problem was getting its planes into the air from a standing start. Many RAAF personnel acted on their own initiative and reported for duty and began planning for the orders they knew would inevitably come. Cos gave them great credit for it and tried to follow his oft-expressed advice that leaders should know when their people are doing a good job and allow them to do it.

> When you spot people doing good things at the outset of the crisis, let them know you are in the picture, shape what they're doing and let them get on with it. No doubt there would have been some fine-tuning a perfectionist might have sought from our preparations and actual deployments, but the essence was in the speed of generating aircraft and at every level people were imbued with that need without encouragement.

He would also warmly applaud the initiative shown by those in Bali.

> . . . by our diplomats in Bali and Jakarta, by young Aussies on holidays who became ad hoc rescue and trauma teams, by Mick Keelty and the police, by our political leaders who may come to count it as one their Government's finest hours in terms of their reaction to the crisis. And may I modestly claim by the young men and women of the ADF who pitched in to play a part. I'm very proud of them.

Cos worked within the convoluted 'diarchy' system in the Australian Defence structure. The CDF commands under the direction of the Minister for Defence and is also the minister's principal military adviser. Under the unique diarchy arrangement, the CDF and the Secretary for the Department of Defence jointly manage the overall Defence organisation. The diarchy arose in the early 1970s when the two previously separate entities, the military forces and the department, were amalgamated into the one organisation. The system reflects the individual responsibilities and accountabilities of both positions. In practice, the diarchy concept cascades through the entire organisation, starting with the adjoining office suites of both chiefs with their immediate staff. The Chief of Staff, Australian Defence HQ/Head Coordination and Public Affairs is responsible equally and directly to both the Secretary and CDF. The two offices work closely on a daily basis, sharing common administration and security systems and having an open interchange of all general correspondence, ministerial submissions and strategic issues. Within the system, the CDF commands the defence forces and advises the minister on military matters while the Secretary is his principal civilian adviser and is the head of the department within the Australian public service. During Cos' time as CDF, Richard Smith was his partner in the diarchy. 'The Secretary, Ric Smith, and I work in a professional marriage. Together we are accountable and responsible for what happens in the defence organisation.'

As David Horner explains, in reality a CDF has extremely limited options should he disagree with the demands of his political leaders.

You've only got two choices when you're the CDF, you either do what the government wants or you resign. You don't have a third choice. Many a senior commander has had to compromise and make that judgement, some rightly and some wrongly. But generally they're better off staying the CDF and doing the best they can than resigning over some particular issue.

And you need to understand that when you're appointed CDF, that you don't have the luxury of saying to the government, for example, I don't think you should be going to Iraq. And you can't be equivocal, you can't say, Yes, but . . . or, Yes, I've got to do it because the government said it, but I don't agree with it. You can't do that. You've got to run with it.

You're seen to be in the government's pocket but that comes from being the CDF. You cannot be anything other than to do what the government says. More junior people can, but not the man who's at the civil, military interface.

David Horner likens the CDF's position to the neck of an hourglass. Above is the whole political governmental apparatus and below is the whole military apparatus. The government delivers its directions to the defence force through the one person, the CDF.

If the government decides it wants to invade Iraq, the Defence Minister says to the CDF, I want you to invade Iraq. The CDF can privately disagree and reply to the minister, I don't think it's a very good idea. And they can argue it out, but once the minister has delivered his decision, the CDF still has only two choices: if he can't stand it, he has to resign; if he doesn't want to resign he's got to salute and carry on and do it.

BACK TO WAR 8

Cos was Commandant of the Infantry Centre and Director of Infantry when, on 2 August 1990, Saddam Hussein first invaded Kuwait and declared it a province of Iraq. The US-led operations, Desert Shield and Desert Storm, sent Hussein's forces packing and by 3 March 1991 Saddam had agreed to a permanent ceasefire. A month later the UN Security Council passed Resolution 687, which allowed Saddam to retain power on the condition that he destroyed all 'weapons of mass destruction'. Until he complied, economic sanctions were to be maintained on Iraq.

Seven years later, Iraq was still refusing to cooperate with the disarmament. In August 1998, it suspended cooperation with the UN weapons inspectors and after negotiations broke down US President Clinton first threatened air strikes scheduled for December and then

signed the *Iraq Liberation Act*, giving financial and organisational support to the anti–Saddam forces within Iraq.

In September 2001 the new President, George W.
Bush, ordered the Pentagon to develop possible war
plans against Iraq. The following January Bush dubbed
Iraq, Iran and North Korea the 'axis of evil' and in-
creased the tempo of preparations for the conflict. That
September he challenged the United Nations to hold
Saddam to his promise to disarm. Congress authorised
Bush to use force in October. On 9 November the UN
Security Council passed Resolution 1441, a rambling,
convoluted series of 'notings' and 'deplorings', which
included:

> Deploring the fact that Iraq has not provided an
> accurate, full, final, and complete disclosure, as
> required by resolution 687 (1991), of all aspects
> of its programmes to develop weapons of mass
> destruction and ballistic missiles with a range
> greater than one hundred and fifty kilometres, and
> of all holdings of such weapons, their components
> and production facilities and locations, as well as
> all other nuclear programmes, including any
> which it claims are for purposes not related to
> nuclear-weapons-usable material . . . demands that
> Iraq confirm within seven days of that notification
> its intention to comply fully with this resolution;
> and demands further that Iraq cooperate im-
> mediately, unconditionally, and actively with
> UNMOVIC and the IAEA.

Still Saddam prevaricated and UN weapons inspector Hans Blix was unable to confirm or deny the existence of the weapons of mass destruction. In January 2003 the United States deployed its first 25,000 troops to the Persian Gulf while France pre-empted Blix's report by announcing it would oppose any moves for war in the United Nations.

Cos farewelled an advance Australian force to the Persian Gulf in late January: the transport ship HMAS *Kanimbla*, carrying 150 SAS troops, an anti-aircraft missile unit and an army explosives disposal team. The force was deployed even while the Howard Government continued to hedge its bets about committing the force to any action against Iraq without UN sanction.

On 13 February, before a shot was fired in anger, Cos was embroiled in a controversy over the inoculation of the members of the force against germ warfare agents such as anthrax. Some sailors from HMAS *Kanimbla* claimed they were intimidated into having the inoculation despite genuine risks to their health. Cos took direct action and largely diffused the issue by arranging to be inoculated himself.

The months dragged on and Saddam stonewalled. In February US Secretary of State Colin Powell addressed the Security Council. In March Bush moved more than 200,000 troops, five carrier groups and 1000 aircraft into place to wage war against Iraq.

Cos had been keeping a watching brief on the events as they unfolded, updated by his network of intelligence, diplomatic, government and international military sources. He spent increasingly long hours preparing for a possible response, well aware of the way the political tides were moving and knowing the government would be seeking his counsel on the most effective contribution the ADF could make to the 'coalition of the willing'.

For months, each day for Cos began at 3.30 am to allow him to get to the 'pit', the war room in the bunker below the Defence Headquarters on Canberra's Russell Hill. Cos would watch events unfold and oversee the massive logistical and operational planning needed. He would still be working late into the night. Cos was always aware of the need for a commander-in-chief to issue overall strategic guidelines and commands and then to allow his commanders on the ground to carry them out without resorting to what the military calls 'the 10,000 mile screwdriver' or interference or micro-management from headquarters, which is now possible, and a constant temptation for some leaders, because of the instant nature of modern communications.

The debate on action against Iraq centred on two crucial issues: one, whether the weapons of mass destruction actually existed; and two, whether the United States and her allies had the right to take military action without the express sanction of the UN Security Council. Bush and his supporters claimed they had intelligence confirming the existence of the weapons and that UN Resolution 1441 gave them sufficient powers to act. Their opponents argued that the UN inspectors should be given more time to complete their task and, in any case, they needed a specific new resolution before they could move on Iraq.

On 13 March John Howard foreshadowed that his Government was seriously considering joining the fight, with or without a new Security Council's sanction, when he spoke on the ABC's *7.30 Report.*

> But I think people do understand that sometimes with these situations if you wait for that additional, beyond-all-doubt, you do end up with a Pearl Harbor situation where something happens and then people say, 'Why on earth didn't you take preventative measures?'

As tensions arose, the British worked feverishly on the diplomatic front to counter the avowed opposition of both France and Russia, while Bush, Blair and the Spanish Prime Minister José Maria Aznar met in the Azores. On 16 March they gave the UN Security Council 24 hours to act against Saddam Hussein. The following day Prime Minister John Howard confirmed what most observers already thought: that war seemed inevitable and that Australian forces would play a role. The United Nations ignored the Bush camp's demand and did nothing. On 17 March Bush issued an ultimatum to Saddam Hussein, giving him 24 hours to leave the country or the United States would take military action. On 18 March Prime Minister Howard committed Australian forces to the conflict. He spoke again to the ABC that same day, justifying his decision.

The whole idea of going back to the Security Council was the hope – this was certainly my view, and I was one of those who encouraged President Bush to go back to the Security Council – was the hope that if you got all the members of the Security Council saying in effect to Iraq, 'Disarm now or we're coming after you,' you might in fact have got a positive response.

But because the Security Council was unable to bring itself to that level of unanimity, that hasn't happened.

Never did I regard going back to the Security Council as being a necessary legal exercise, I made that clear in my statement to the Parliament on 4 February and when I said we didn't need the 18th resolution of the Security Council on this subject in order to get more legal cover, rather to increase the level of international pressure on Iraq.

One hour after the deadline passed the United States began bombarding Baghdad with cruise missiles and artillery. The Australian involvement was numerically small, but tactically important. Australia's SAS had effectively moved to Iraq straight from Afghanistan. As a result of the reputation the Aussies established in Afghanistan the Americans entrusted them with a critical role in the Iraqi conflict, Operation Falconer, the suppression of Iraqi scud launchers, which the Americans feared would be fired from the western region of Iraq into Israel. The task was vital because Israel had threatened to respond with nuclear weapons. The SAS went into action on the first day of the conflict, achieving its aim of neutralising the Iraqi weapons.

Cos had long admired his 'chicken stranglers' and was especially proud of their achievements in Iraq. While maintaining their anonymity, he made sure some of their achievements came to public notice, like Trooper X's heroism during Operation Falconer.

Trooper X's patrol was clearing an Iraqi installation believed to control ballistic missiles. As the machine-gunner, exposed in the mounting ring of his armoured patrol vehicle, Trooper X found himself confronting an Iraqi special operations force of two vehicles and up to 20 heavily armed troops. Under withering fire he destroyed the first Iraqi vehicle with a Javelin missile. When the Aussies charged the Iraqis Trooper X held off a supporting Iraqi position with his machine gun and then switched back to his Javelin system and destroyed the second enemy vehicle. The Iraqis tried to set up a mortar position but Trooper X picked up his sniper's rifle and, with his first round, hit and exploded the mortar tube. With superb marksmanship he targeted the Iraqis, who were still fighting from cover, and forced them to surrender. He was awarded the Medal for Gallantry. His citation read in part:

Throughout this engagement, Trooper X demonstrated skills and composure of the highest standard. He acted with very little direction and his decisions and subsequent actions had significant impacts on the outcome of the engagement. His actions in destroying the enemy vehicles gave the Australian forces freedom of movement and put the Iraqi forces under immediate pressure. For the entire engagement, Trooper X was subject to enemy fire passing close overhead. He readily accepted the personal danger and disregarded his own safety while acquiring the enemy vehicles with the Javelin. His conduct whilst in a hazardous situation in contact with numerically superior enemy forces was most gallant and led to the success of the action.

★ ★ ★

By 26 March Cos was able to report that our troops were safe and performing admirably. Australian divers were clearing Umm Qasr port so it could receive allied humanitarian aid ships and had already successfully found and destroyed mines. HMAS *Anzac* and *Darwin* were supporting the Royal Marines on the Al-Faw Peninsula. The SAS was conducting successful long-range reconnaissance patrols, feeding back intelligence and intercepting Iraqi troop movements. And the RAAF Hercules and Chinooks were ferrying supplies around the theatre almost non-stop.

In June 2003 Cos addressed the Sydney Institute and reflected on what he saw as the essential elements of his role as CDF, in addition to his roles as the senior military adviser to the government and the commander of the armed forces.

I also have a very strong moral obligation to the mums and dads of Australia. Through my decisions and orders, I have to expose their sons and daughters to the inevitable risks of military action while also giving the highest possible consideration to their wellbeing. These are the differences between an academic strategic perspective and a soldier's perspective.

This view was consistent with the approach Cos took during his time as CDF. His genuine affection for the digger was reinforced by the rare, but keenly enjoyed, opportunities he got to talk to his troops.

When I get an opportunity to talk to them at any length, a length more than two or three minutes, after the guy's got over the culture shock of talking to a general, after just a very short time, they think, 'Well, this guy's not going to bite my head off' and you start having a bit of a gossip. The years fall away from me and I could be a young and quite confident young officer.

So, I'll never lapse back to being perhaps the brand new boy, but I feel in conversation with the soldiers that the years have gone away and I'm talking to the same sort of diggers as I knew so well when I was a young officer.

And the same sort of things get up their nose: people mucking them about; giving them four or five different versions of what's going to happen next; being treated like mushrooms – where's my mail; would be nice if we could get a hot meal hot and a cold drink cold; who's the idiot who designed the 'no gear' policy. Among others it was probably me! The thing I find about soldiers too is if you can talk to them about what you want to do and why you're doing it, why you're asking them to do it, even if you're any number of ranks removed from them, which I tend to be these days, they appreciate it. So they don't want you to run round sort of babying them to make them happy. They hate to be taken for granted and not told why, which is obviously hard, but it needs to be done that way.

So to me it's a two-way street where you prise these characteristics out of diggers, then you've got to acknowledge them in the way you actually relate to them. Very few martinets, authoritarian sorts of popinjays, flourish in the army. Not just the soldiers but also the other leaders in the army sort of don't like that style and somebody will either adjust their style or find a different employment.

★ ★ ★

Cos found himself at the helm when the ADF was adapting to deal with the emergence of new and growing threats: transnational crime and the stresses it placed on border security and the ever-morphing spectre of international terrorism. The ADF expanded its Sydney-based Special Operations Command and reinforced the Incident Response Regiment that it created for the Sydney Olympics. Its task was to liaise with civilian organisations to deal with chemical, biological and radiological and other similar threats posed by terrorists.

Cos also explored and expanded the state-of-the-art system known as Network-Centric Warfare which used satellite and web-based technology to achieve strategic and tactical information dominance. As he explained to the Sydney Institute:

> By this I mean that we know more than an adversary and we know that we know more.
>
> When this occurs it is a moot point whether the adversary knows that we know more than him. Some theorists think it is good for him to appreciate his inferiority. Others think his ignorance is our further bliss.
>
> Essentially, though, this knowledge edge is the prerequisite to using force precisely, economically, minimally, discriminately and decisively.

The system was used to great effect in Iraq. It enabled the US-led forces to avoid risky large-scale conventional battles and allowed them to comprehensively outmanoeuvre and defeat the Iraqis' main forces in just four weeks. That the conflict lingered on subsequently was largely because the US forces there were insufficient in numbers to achieve the expanded political objectives set by the Bush administration.

For his part, Cos had learned the lessons of East

Timor, in terms of preparation and logistics, and had planned for a limited and finite engagement of his combat troops. He succeeded in his aims. He did this by ensuring that the Australians became involved early in the planning with the Americans. That enabled him to secure an agreement that his forces would have responsibility for specific territory while there. From their side, the Americans were happy for a trusted partner to take responsibility. By adopting this approach Cos was able to substantially reduce the prospect of Australian casualties. By advising the government that, should it decide to become involved, a short-term combat commitment was prudent, the ADF was able to make a relatively clean withdrawal of its combat elements after the initial stages of the conflict without casualties or the risks of prolonged exposure in the aftermath.

The strategy enabled Prime Minister Howard to state our conditions of involvement as effectively being, 'We're in at the beginning but when the fight is over, we're out.' The Americans, keen to begin the engagement, were in no position to argue. And that's how it ended. Cos was able to withdraw Australia's Hornet fighters, the SAS group and RAN mine clearance divers. Australia maintained a presence with ships and Orion aircraft to patrol the northern regions of the Gulf, some Hercules for transports and a security detachment. The Australian troop commitment dropped from about 1200 to around 400. It was a performance that won praise from Professor David Horner.

I think the whole thing was extremely well managed. I'm not making a judgement on whether we should or should not have gone into Iraq. I'm just talking purely in a technical sense – the management of this thing. It was General Cosgrove's real achievement in a strategic sense. It was managed well and without a casualty.

He understands about command and about operations and how to manage operations in the modern era with the management of information. To enable him to respond accurately to the government, he put in place arrangements where he spoke directly to his commanders and then he talked to the government and so that there could be no breakdown of communications there.

One of the problems with the children overboard affair was a breakdown in communications. To solve this, defence set up a sophisticated computer system, with a pull-down menu, so that commanders at various levels can get visibility to what was going on.

So then it would be possible for the field commander at his computer terminal to click on this thing, pull it up and have a look at it and therefore if Cosgrove had said to the government that such and such is happening, and there was a mistake, the commander could say, Oh, it's wrong. And he could get straight back to Cosgrove and say, No, that's not right, such and such is. So it gives a great deal more visibility.

When Cos took over as CDF, this system was sitting in his 'to do' pile on his desk. It had been explored by General Ken Gillespie and was awaiting approval and funding. Cos saw its merit and gave it the go-ahead. With it, he could sit at his desk and plug into top-secret menus that allowed him to be on top of the latest information on the course of the war, and thus be in a position to pass that information on to his minister.

By May 2003 Cos was speaking glowingly of his Network-Centric Warfare at a conference on the subject in Sydney and using Iraq as an example of how the new information-age warfare would in the future 'coexist with the cruder aspects of industrial or even pre-industrial warfare'.

> While it is likely that some type of crude kinetic effect will still be the ultimate expression of violence in war, it is also likely that as information and network-related war fighting techniques start to mature and to predominate, outcomes will be swifter, as dramatic and paradoxically less bloody than the classic force-on-force attritionist para-digm of the past.
>
> What I have euphemistically called 'kinetic effect' – blast, heat and penetrating metal was witnessed in abundance in the media coverage of the Iraq war. But in the main, the Iraqi forces were beaten quickly, spectacularly and comprehensively by a force using what were, on balance, mostly first-generation network-centric technologies and

concepts. The very nature of this dimension of the war was at once both much more difficult to convey and less spectacular too, but ironically, absolutely in evidence at every hand in the media's networking of its own operations.

Cos pointed out that the system gathered humint (intelligence from spies using mobile phones) that allowed coalition Special Forces and aircraft to conduct raids, with a reaction time reduced from days down to minutes, even though the basic technology hadn't advanced greatly for almost a decade.

RAN ships used a newly upgraded Naval intranet, incorporating ship-to-ship chat rooms, which allowed them to update situations in seconds. It was directly responsible for preventing the Iraqis from releasing mines into the gulf in the early days of the war. Cos gave a special preview of what he called 'Generation One of Network-Centric Warfare – the Australian way':

Our first 'battle', so to speak, of the war was to get satellite bandwidth. We needed enough into and out of the Gulf to be able to pass quick, accurate, high-density data 24 hours a day. Once we had 'won' (basically bought!) enough bandwidth, we were able to network our Command and Control system from the strategic, through the operational to the senior tactical level.

We used as a major tool an Operation Bastille (the forward deployment of our troops) home page and then for the war itself an Operation Falconer homepage. To these was posted a huge variety of information, vetted, catalogued and updated and archived, throughout the operation.

Everybody in the staff and command chain had access to virtually the entire database and could browse or do focused reference to particular issues. For me, the first two hours of a relatively long day were spent poring over the website reading the various reports, following up on them by email, by telephone and face to face.

Conversely, Brigadier Maurie McNarn, in command on the ground in the Middle East, could read Australian intelligence reports immediately they were posted on the system. And Cos could track the SAS's movements to within metres with GPS links and could even view digital photos as they worked. But well aware of the increased reach of his now digital 10,000 mile screwdriver, Cos was at pains to resist the urge to micro-manage.

You will be relieved to know that I refrained from bombarding these magnificent troops with orders from my level, although I didn't hesitate to send my congratulations and encouragement down through the chain of command. The point is though, that the occasion, the means and the opportunity can come together to allow a tactical element to foreshadow and to achieve a strategic outcome, a situation improbable in warfare up until the information age in which we now live.

The complexity of Cos' work as CDF was well illustrated by the extensive deployment of his forces as at October 2003 – more than 3600 people on 12 operations, regionally and around the world. In addition to Operation Catalyst, the continuing support forces in Iraq, these included Operation Belisi in Bougainville, Operation Citadel supporting the United Nations in East Timor, Operation Bali Assist in the aftermath of the bombing and Operation Anode in the Solomon Islands.

By December 2003, the emphasis of media and public scrutiny of Australia's Iraqi involvement had switched to the lack of weapons of mass destruction, the central pretext for the invasion. On his third visit to his troops in Iraq, Cos found himself defending the position.

I think it's important that we are patient and assiduous and energetic in our assistance that we provide for this particular part of the post-war investigations of what took place in Iraq before the war phase.

I think you've just got to keep looking for answers. Very plainly there was a great suspicion that there was a substantial set of programs of weapons of mass destruction here, and I think it's important that we continue to explore that aspect until everybody's confident in the final answers.

... I don't think you can typify any sort of

modern conflict. This one is unique. The aftermath is unique. What is important, though, is that
the international community rehabilitates Iraq.

★ ★ ★

By February 2004 the personnel on deployment had
dropped to around 2000 troops deployed on ten operations: 850 people still on Operation Catalyst in Iraq,
about 500 on Operation Anode in the Solomons and
around 440 troops in East Timor as part of United
Nations Mission of Support in East Timor (UNMISET),
and the remainder on peacekeeping duties in the Middle
East, Eritrea and Ethiopia and Afghanistan, with military
liaison officers in coalition headquarters and diplomatic
missions around the world.

THE COLLINS AFFAIR 9

The curious story of what became known as the Collins Affair shadowed Cos during the last five years of his service. It began with what seemed like a technical glitch in East Timor in December 1999. It ended with a series of inquiries and counter-inquiries that highlighted some disturbing cultural and systemic problems in Australia's military, bureaucracy, government and intelligence services.

The figure at the centre of the controversy was a career soldier, a respected intelligence officer with a recognised specialty in South-East Asia. Lieutenant Colonel Lance Collins graduated from La Trobe University before entering the ADF's Officer Cadet School at Portsea in 1979. (Ironically, in the light of subsequent events, there Collins won the Everard Baillieu Prize for studies associated with Australia's role in Asia.) He was commissioned a lieutenant and, after serving as an infantry platoon commander, moved into intelligence. During a two-year electronic warfare posting outside Toowoomba he met and worked with a fellow officer named Mervyn Jenkins who would play a tragic role in the overall story many years later. From Toowoomba, Collins was transferred to the Indonesian desk at the Joint Intelligence Organisation in Canberra. It would be a fateful posting, as Collins would later reflect:

> The army just posted me to the Indonesian section. It wasn't me putting my hand up to join the Indonesian industry or anything like that. I didn't have any leaning towards it at that stage, I was aware of Timor, I knew about Timor ponies and things since I was a kid.
>
> I was at university when the invasion of East Timor happened. And I think like any ordinary Australian I don't like to see your neighbours cut up. Just sympathy for the underdog and there's no doubt the occupation was brutal so I was sympathetic but I wasn't connected.

Collins arrived at the Indonesian desk in 1986, in the days of a new Australian rapport with Indonesia. The prevailing dogma in the place was that the Indonesians were doing their best in East Timor, building roads and schools and infrastructure, and that the resistance would dissipate once all the kids had been taught Bahasa (Indonesian) and the older generation had lost its influence. Collins wasn't so sure. He had studied anthropology at university and began going back to first principles, starting with anthropological studies from the Portuguese days in Timor, extending this initial research to everything he could find on the 1975 Indonesian occupation. He came to a different conclusion to his department's prevailing view. He believed the occupation was brutal and that the resistance would continue for a long time. 'For that I got branded as not being able to see the other person's point of view and anti-Indonesian.'

Collins' different viewpoint did not hold back his career within the service. His performance assessments were above average and his promotion path was on track. He even rode through a controversial intelligence estimate on East Timor he co-authored in 1998. (Although, in retrospect, Collins believes his trouble may have begun with the Defence Intelligence Organisation (DIO) censures against him dating back to this report.) The report was ordered by Collins' then boss. An intelligence estimate calls for an examination and analysis of the historical background and the current situation to deliver predictions of likely future events. Collins' report warned that the East Timorese pro-independence movement would continue and grow in strength; that the TNI (the Indonesian military) would likely foment violence in East Timor should there be an independence vote; that the TNI and the local militia were essentially one and the same; and that Australia would likely be involved in a UN-sponsored peacekeeping force should the violence occur. These predictions would later be proved correct. The most contentious element in Collins' report was his claim of the existence of a 'pro-Jakarta lobby' that prevented accurate assessments being sent to or heard within government.

Despite rolling these hand grenades into the defence intelligence establishment, Collins was appointed as the senior intelligence officer at the headquarters of Cos' Deployable Joint Force in Brisbane. Prior to his appointment there Collins had never met Cos, but the two men struck up an easy working relationship and enjoyed exploring their mutual interest in history.

In the prelude to the DJF's move as the main component of INTERFET, Collins learned of moves, instigated from Canberra and made without informing him directly, to try to prevent him going to East Timor as the Force Intelligence Officer. He attributes them to a classified paper he wrote around the time, named 'Beyond Credulity', which repeated his assertions that 'pro-Jakarta' elements were skewing their assessments about Indonesia and East Timor.

Cos recalled chatting to Collins and questioning whether he really wanted to send the report because it was so inflammatory, as he later told RAN Captain Martin Toohey (who was appointed in 2003 to investigate Collins' grievances): 'My impression is of having had the discussion with Lance, "Oh this is pretty red hot, mate, are you sure you want to send this?"' Collins sent the report. The moves to oust him were over-ridden by the Force's Headquarters and he went to East Timor as Cos' top intelligence officer.

As always, Cos studied every aspect of his assignment as he prepared for the deployment. Collins briefed Cos with all the assessments and other intelligence material he could find. He even lent Cos, early in 1999, his copy of Bernard Callinan's *Independent Company*, the classic account of the Sparrow Force heroic fight behind enemy lines in Timor during World War II. Collins was impressed with Cos' grasp of detail and believed that he agreed, in essence, with his assessments of the situation.

By all accounts, including Cos', Collins performed admirably in East Timor, providing a steady and reliable flow of vital intelligence to the forces on the ground. (Even while defending the DIO's performance when he was CDF in April 2004 on the ABC Radio's *AM* program Cos still spoke glowingly of Collins and his work in East Timor. 'Lance Collins is a great officer. He did great work for me and for all the people he supported in East Timor, and from my point of view I'd listen very carefully to anything he says.' This backed up his evidence, given in his interview with Captain Toohey: 'Lance did very well in East Timor. He did very well under great pressures of warlike service, producing crucial combat and other operational intelligence for force protection and to help achieve the INTERFET mission.')

The trigger point for the Collins Affair occurred on 20 December 1999, when someone pulled the plug on

INTERFET's access to Australia's top-secret intelligence database, TOPIC, and kept them offline for more than 24 hours. It happened at a very difficult time in Dili, on the very day Cos had written to his Indonesian counterparts expressing his concern that the security situation at the border between East and West Timor was deteriorating. The attacks on INTERFET forces in the area had prompted Cos to chopper up another 100 troops to try to gain control. By any interpretation, the interruption to intelligence increased the risks to Cos' men and to those for whom they were responsible – the UN staff, AFP personnel, aid workers and civilians.

A few weeks earlier the Australian intelligence group at INTERFET headquarters in Dili had switched from their original US-deployed and -manned communications system to the Australian Joint Intelligence Support (JIS) system, allowing the Americans to head home in time for Christmas. While INTERNET's intelligence cell had operated under the US-facilitated ABCA system (Australian, British, Canadian, American), Canberra could not control the flow of material that was posted via the US Pacific Command server based out of Hawaii. This clearly irked Canberra. Collins later claimed DIO cut off crucial intelligence to troops on the ground for 24 hours because it wanted to regain control of what was reported about Indonesia by the international force. As Collins told the Toohey Inquiry:

> At one stage we were cut off from top-secret intelligence by DIO, who gave contradictory

explanations about why that was so, and it wasn't turned back on until I had certified to them that I had conveyed a minute from (Frank) Lewincamp, the Director of DIO, to the Force Commander, General Cosgrove, directing us not to report on events to the west of the East Timor/West Timor border.

Cos responded to Toohey:

That's intriguing because I can't remember sighting a minute from Lewincamp. Now, there was a period when we had difficulties with the volume of high classification material we were getting, and we wondered whether they'd gone silent in Canberra or whether we weren't getting all that we wanted. And I recall discussing with Lance and some of my senior staff, and also discussing with, I think, Major General Keating, who was then the Head of Strategic Operations Division, or Strategic Command Division as it was called then.

For his part, Collins claimed a very clear recollection of giving Lewincamp's letter to Cos. He gave evidence to this effect on oath to the Senate. Collins said that he told Cos they had unintentionally upset DIO and passed him Lewincamp's letter. He said Cos read it at his desk, leaned back in his chair, waved his arm in an easygoing manner and said, 'Rockets all round. I don't know what is wrong with you intelligence people, insisting on thinking for yourselves.' The meeting concluded with a short and amiable conversation about getting things working again.

Cos went on to tell Toohey:

So I recall this period and it would probably have been late 2000, late 1999. I can't recall, but won't deny that there was a minute from Lewincamp. Now, on the issue, even if there was a minute my inclination was to adjust as necessary and get on with the show. I specifically can't recall any prohibitions or advice not to worry about what was happening in West Timor. This part would be classified that I'm talking about . . . if we sort of knew stuff that was happening in West Timor we'd report it.

On his return from Timor in late February 2000, Collins heard through his sources that the knives were out for him. Back at his post at the Joint Deployable Force Headquarters in Brisbane, he remained vigilant. At this stage Cos had been appointed Land Commander in Sydney.

Collins worked uninterrupted until 21 September 2000, when he received a shattering phone call from his former wife. His name had been revealed on the front page of *The Sydney Morning Herald* as being on a Federal Police search warrant used to search the house of the then Captain Clinton Fernandes in an investigation into alleged defence intelligence leaks. Collins was furious.

He was an officer who, for more than 20 years, had access to the most secret and sensitive material without blemish. He had no idea why he would have been implicated in any investigation. He wanted an explanation, and he wanted an apology.

Collins waited in vain and in December 2000 he wrote a letter of complaint to the Minister for Defence about the conduct of the investigation into the suicide in June 1999 of Mervyn Jenkins, DIO attaché in Washington, the shortcomings of Australian strategic intelligence, including the cut-off of intelligence to INTERFET and the sympathy of some quarters of government to Indonesian foreign policy. The Minister referred the complaint to the Inspector-General of Intelligence and Security, Bill Blick.

Blick took three years to complete an 11-page report that found, by relying on sworn statements from DIO officials and in contradiction to documentary evidence it presented, that the loss of intelligence access in East Timor was caused by technical problems, not by a deliberate decision.

Collins wasn't exactly surprised. He knew this to be untrue. When he'd been alerted to the original problem on 20 December 1999, Collins and his team had initially assumed that it was a technical fault. When they checked the system out, they found no problems. Collins rang Canberra and was told they had been cut off.

In April 2003 Collins' patience ran out and he made a soldier's 'Redress of Grievance' request under the ADF's internal system. By that stage he had lost faith in the army and asked that an officer from another service conduct the investigation. The army commissioned a respected naval lawyer, Captain Martin Toohey, to conduct an inquiry into Collins' claims. Toohey had spent more than 30 years in the RAN, including security appointments, the last six in the Naval Reserve while working as a civilian barrister and solicitor and court administrator. He was well respected in both sides of his career. Within four months he delivered his report.

The report was handed to the army on 7 September 2003. It sat for more than six months. Subsequent revelations, particularly by *The Bulletin*'s John Lyons, revealed that the ADF's inner sanctum had dived for cover when they read the report.

Toohey had concluded:

I find as a fact that the Defence Security Branch (activated, on the balance of probabilities) by malice, at the material time failed to inform Lieutenant Colonel Collins as soon as practicable after the execution of the AFP search warrant of the fact that he was not, and never had been under investigation . . . I find as a fact that the incident could have been prevented by the Assistant Secretary-Defence Secretary, Mr Jason Browne, advising Lieutenant Colonel Collins, in a timely manner, of the complainant's complete lack of involvement in the security investigation.

The report went on to drop another grenade,

concluding that DIO Chief Frank Lewincamp 'caused the flow of intelligence to East Timor to be suspended for approximately 24 hours'.

Collins' attempts to gain access to Toohey's report were met with a series of periodic progress reports that said he would be advised in due course. In March 2004, after waiting for six months without success, Collins wrote directly to the Prime Minister. On 14 April 2004 *The Bulletin* published key extracts of the Toohey Report, again throwing both the Prime Minister's Department and the Defence Department into spins as they decided how to diffuse the situation.

Perhaps in the light of the public backlash that followed an earlier attempt to 'play the man' when they attacked AFP Commissioner Mick Keelty for a statement about Australia's increased security risks following involvement in Iraq, they took another well-trodden path: they tried to discredit the author of the report. They sought a number of opinions trying to counter it. Despite a flurry of spin-doctoring, the true sequence of events was eventually clarified during a penetrating interview of Defence Minister Senator Robert Hill by the host of ABC TV's *Lateline* program, Tony Jones, on 14 April 2004.

The minister had planned to use the program to talk up a report he'd released earlier in the day in an attempt to 'trump' the Toohey Report. The new report was by another Army Reserve lawyer, Melbourne QC Richard Tracey. Tracey found 'there can be no doubt there have been shortcomings in his [Collins'] career management since his return from East Timor', but he concluded that the Toohey Report had 'miscarried' as it had led to an investigation of 'bodies external to the ADF and insofar as it has led to recommendations for action by you which you could not, lawfully, take'.

But Tony Jones knew that there were three reports dealing with Collins, not two. When he confronted Senator Hill with this small detail the game was up. The minister was forced to admit to the other report written by Colonel Roger Brown, a Sydney magistrate and reservist who held a PhD in law from Cambridge. Senator Hill also acknowledged that the Brown Report was the second report and that it had effectively backed up Toohey's findings. The third report, by Colonel Tracey, was sought only after Brown had concluded:

> Captain Toohey's inquiry was in accordance with his terms of reference . . . It should be noted it is a vital element of both legal and intelligence work that advisers be free to tender their advice, whether popular or not, without fear of repercussions for failing 'to toe the party line'. Captain Toohey's findings clearly demonstrate that Lt Col Collins was denied this freedom.

The minister tried to categorise Brown's report as only being 'a process matter'. But Brown had specifically said that his review had 'necessitated a very close examination of the supporting documents to ensure they are accurately reported' and went on to add, 'There is no apparent defect in the appointment process or the report itself'. Finally Hill recommended that Toohey's Report be given to Collins.

The minister's attempt to defuse the situation failed lamentably. The situation lapsed into farce when yet another leak revealed another example of the obsession with secrecy. The leak involved an email from Colonel Gary Hogan, the man Cos had appointed as the liaison officer to the ongoing Senate Inquiry into Military Justice. The email asked that:

> All inquiry-related correspondence should be headed 'Internal Working Document' in order that the correspondence be exempt from tabling before the Committee under the Freedom of Information Act.

In April 2004 Martin Toohey called for a Royal Commission into Australia's intelligence services, claiming he had been subjected to 'a witch-hunt' over his report. He claimed that his and Collin's concerns about bias in the agencies were supported by classified intelligence reports and the evidence of other current senior officers. Toohey was twice investigated by Defence Security officers over the leaking of his report to *The Bulletin*. 'I have no idea how it was leaked, I told them so. They didn't appear to have any authority to be interviewing me. Now, that's simply not good enough. It's a witch-hunt and don't shoot the messenger, really.'

Toohey believes the problem is endemic and cites

many individual cases in which he has been involved where the system had failed servicemen and -women and their families.

> This has been a constant thorn in my side, in my long career in the navy, but there's been no follow-up. Affected people such as husbands, fathers, mothers have been left in the dark and not told what the results of the boards of inquiry have been.

Responding on ABC radio program *AM* on 20 April 2004, Cos backed the findings of the third review by Richard Tracey.

> I was aware at the time that there was a temporary disconnect on our communications, but I think if I refer you to Colonel Tracey's report at page 10, paragraph 14 and following, you'll see that the IGIS [Inspector-General of Intelligence Security] concluded that there was a technical breakdown on one part, and then there was another break-down to do with a procedural issue, which had no sinister overtones.

Later in the interview Cos was at pains to explain that he felt that the issue was confined to two dissident officers and did not extend further.

> I'm anxious to ensure that in all of this, people

don't say that they're somehow weaselling their way round, writing briefs to suit governments. That hasn't happened in my time, and I don't expect it'll happen in the future.

On 22 April 2004, Cos and his diarchy partner, the Secretary of the Department of Defence, Ric Smith, wrote a letter to the editor of *The Australian*, which they said was to 'point out' that the 'central theme' of an article written the previous day by journalist Janet Albrechtsen '. . . that the flow of intelligence to Australian forces in East Timor was deliberately cut off by the Director of the Defence Intelligence Organisation (DIO) has no basis in fact.'

The letter went on:

There was never any cut to the overall intelligence flow to forces in East Timor, nor were the lives of Australian personnel endangered.

One of the intelligence systems supporting the forces in East Timor was a prototype system, which, amongst other things, provided access to a specific DIO database. That prototype system was being made available to deployed forces for the first time, and suffered technical problems and a number of outages.

On one occasion in December 1999, when the forces in East Timor lost access to that specific DIO database for a short period, Lieu-tenant Colonel Collins was told that this was a

DIO policy decision. That was not, in fact, the case and he was so advised immediately. The Director DIO wrote to both General Cosgrove and Lieutenant Colonel Collins the next day explaining the circumstances surrounding the outage.

There is simply no basis for the finding by Captain Toohey that the Director DIO caused the flow of intelligence to be suspended.

As stated publicly and reported by the media this week, the matter has been investigated and we are thoroughly satisfied with the results of those investigations, which are detailed above.

The defence intelligence agencies are professional organisations staffed by skilled military and civilian personnel. Among their very highest priorities is that of supporting our men and women in the field. Any suggestion that they or their leaders would place in jeopardy the safety of our troops is repugnant.

This unequivocal response to Collins' claims carried great weight. All the more so because Cos was his commander in East Timor at the time of the cut in the flow of intelligence. The fact that Cos and Smith took the unusual step of responding publicly to *The Australian*'s story also added further weight.

When asked by the media what those who disagreed with intelligence being disseminated by DIO should do, Cos played a rigidly straight bat and suggested they do the same.

> Well, they should take up their concerns in a
> reasonable way, and they should use logic to
> explain what it is that they have at issue, and then
> get into the process as they would do it. I mean,
> I'm certainly not looking in any way to see
> anybody stifled. I do see, though, that in the end,
> umpires give decisions and then you take your bat
> under your arm and you walk off the wicket.

There are others who believe that the system should
follow cricket into the new age and introduce the equivalent of the independent 'third umpire' with the benefit
of slow-motion replays. In any event, Cos defended the
DIO's performance.

> The Defence Intelligence Organisation has been
> doing a fantastic job over the last several years,
> and I think the results speak for themselves. My
> concern is under the present miasma of innuendo
> and suggestion that they are somehow partial, that
> they'll lose that viable edge they need to keep our
> men and women safe, and I won't have that.

He was content with Collins' treatment at that time.

> He's already had a hearing to a pretty high degree
> on these issues when he referred these issues
> to the Inspector-General of Intelligence and

Security. And I noticed at the time that, as I expected the IGIS found that Lance had those honestly held, sincerely felt and profoundly felt beliefs, but he could not give them any objective credit.

In an example of the cynical methods that have characterised the Government's approach to the entire affair, the Minister for Defence, Senator Hill, tried to bury the results of a fourth inquiry into Collins' claims by tabling it on the final parliamentary sitting day on 10 December 2004. Bill Blick's successor as Inspector-General of Intelligence and Security, Ian Carnell, conducted the inquiry and wrote to the minister in November confirming that Collins' claim that the flow of intelligence to Australian troops was deliberately shut down for more than 24 hours had been true.

Carnell had written to the minister confirming Collins' claims that the intelligence had been deliberately turned off, after Collins had found out what was afoot, and pre-emptively written to both Carnell and Senator Hill. On 22 November, Collins wrote to Carnell that he had learned that Carnell's inquiries had revealed:

> ... that a senior public service officer did order the top secret intelligence link to Headquarters International Force East Timor to be cut off; this instruction was relayed to a second DIO officer, who passed it on to a subordinate; the third person in this chain gave the direct order that

the link be cut; to a fourth DIO of JISS Project Officer, who executed the cut.

However, Carnell denied the cut was done on the orders of Frank Lewincamp, offering the explanation that it followed security concerns to protect certain categories of intelligence and to limit the use of the database. He claimed the loss of access 'did not seem to have been a critical deficiency in operational terms'.

Despite this about-face by Carnell, neither Cos nor Ric Smith has ever corrected or retracted their earlier incorrect assertion that Collins was wrong and there was 'no basis' for his claim that the loss of access was deliberate.

Lance Collins is still waiting for a proper resolution of the affair. He and Martin Toohey, two respected and honourable men, have had their careers irreparably damaged and suffered overt and covert attempts at character assassination.

Perhaps it's the nature of the beast, as Norman F. Dixon points out in his excellent book *On the Psychology of Military Incompetence*, that throughout history many leaders have chosen:

> '. . . honourable ignorance' over 'useful knowledge gained by devious means'. The history of the various departments of espionage and counter-espionage, of 'special operations' and the like, is one of badly staffed, ill-equipped Cinderella organisations struggling to perform their duties in

the face of contempt, jealousy and resentment from army and navy service chiefs.

The internationally respected Australian journalist and author Phillip Knightley put it simply, as quoted in *The Sydney Morning Herald* on 23 May 2004: 'Even though Lieutenant Colonel Lance Collins, probably the best and brightest military intelligence officer this country has produced, got it right, no one would listen to him.'

THE FINAL
SALUTE 10

Speaking to the students at the Higher Command and
Staff Studies Course in November 2004, Cos revealed his
acute understanding of the operation of the media and
gave an insight into his thinking on the vital role of what
he called 'public affairs'.

> I cannot stress enough the importance of main-
> taining the support of the Australian people for
> ADF operations and, ultimately, for the ADF itself.
> Such support is central to our operational success.
> It is for this reason that I have made public affairs
> a central responsibility of command and ensured
> that there is an integrated public affairs staff in
> planning headquarters.

Cos was determined to wage a public-affairs campaign that was as 'sophisticated as any other part of our operational planning and more complex than most' and he highlighted its role in both Iraq and the Solomons. He warned the attendees, all potential senior commanders, not to think they could 'manage' the media but rather to accept its role and to concentrate on presenting 'a consistent and credible face to the world'. He gave this prescient advice.

> Remember that media reporting of a major incident in an area of operations will often reach the Prime Minister before I have been fully informed by the operational chain. We are unlikely to beat the media – so we had better have more comprehensive and reliable information, otherwise the perceived value of military advice to government will be in jeopardy.

In late June 2003, Cos found himself in controversial waters with the discovery of illegal drug use at Lavarack Barracks in Townsville. It would be the start of a series of events that would force him on to the back foot and draw him into the murky world of politics. Responding in the media, Cos said:

> People are realistic enough to know that when there is temptation proliferating in the whole community, from time to time even our magnificent young men and women will occasionally fall

to temptations. What we've got to do is make sure that everyone understands that it is not tolerated and we'll jump on it.

Two months later, media reports revealed that the ADF had reopened links with Kopassus, the Indonesian Special Forces that had emerged from the East Timor crisis under a cloud. Cos justified the move as the only sensible way to work together with the Indonesians in combating terrorism in the light of the Bali bombings. 'They are at the moment the force in Indonesia who would assist Australians if they were under that sort of threat in Indonesia.'

Then, out of the blue, Cos found himself embroiled in what became known as 'The Keelty Affair'. On 14 March 2004, in an interview on Channel Nine's *Sunday* program, host Jana Wendt asked AFP Commissioner Mick Keelty whether a 'Madrid-type' bombing (where a terrorist train bombing had killed 190 people) could happen in Australia. He answered:

Well, I think we've said all along this is an uphill battle. This is a marathon, not a sprint. The reality is, if this turns out to be Islamic extremists responsible for this bombing in Spain, it's more likely to be linked to the position that Spain and other allies took on issues such as Iraq. And I don't think anyone's been hiding the fact that we do believe that ultimately one day, whether it be in one month's time, one year's time, or ten years' time, something will happen.

And no one can guarantee it won't. And I think there's a level of honesty that has to exist here in terms of what the problems are here, not only in Australia but in our region.

But, on the threat level, the threat level here in Australia hasn't changed. It still remains at medium. It has been at medium for some time for an attack on Australians in Australia.

This was a bombshell, coming from Mick Keelty. When Mick Keelty made a statement on terrorism, people listened. And if he said that 'if this turns out to be Islamic extremists responsible for this bombing in Spain, it's more likely to be linked to the position that Spain and other allies took on issues such as Iraq', then people gave it great weight.

Keelty's public profile and the esteem in which he was held had risen greatly because of his work during the 2002 Bali bombings. Under his stewardship, in the years following the 9/11 terrorist attacks in the United States and Bali, the Australian Federal Police had grown to meet the challenges of international terrorism and transnational crime, with its personnel doubling to more than 5000 and its budget almost quadrupling to around $1 billion.

To many Australians, Keelty's answer seemed to be a statement of the obvious. But Prime Minister Howard had listened to Keelty's statement and he didn't like what he heard. He and his government had been promoting the line that Australia's involvement in the military intervention in Iraq had not made it a greater target because the terrorists already hated what Australia stood for. The political ramifications of Keelty's statement to the Government's credibility were obvious. The Government reacted by setting the dogs on Keelty, with the Prime Minister's Chief of Staff, Arthur Sindonis, leading the charge even before Keelty had left the television station.

Then Prime Minister Howard came out the next day saying:

> There is no direct link between what has occurred in Spain and Australia. It is my very strong view, and the view of the majority of experts in this area, that we are a terrorist target because of who we are, rather than because of what we have done.

He also pointed out that ASIO's assessment was that the main suspect for the Madrid bombing, al-Qaeda, did not see Iraq as 'particularly relevant' to its intent or purpose. Attorney General Philip Ruddock chimed in that there was no evidence to support Keelty's claim, while on 16 March Foreign Minister Alexander Downer upped the ante.

> I mean, he's said what he's said, and I think that you're overstating, you're overstating what he actually said. I mean I think he is just expressing a view which reflects a lot of the propaganda we're

getting from al-Qaeda, I think the bottom line of all of this is that al-Qaeda are out there running this line on Iraq.

But, most disturbingly for Mick Keelty, Cos also came forward to contradict him. At a doorstep interview with media in Canberra, Cos was asked, 'I'm wondering if you think we're at greater risk of a terrorist attack after Iraq?' He replied:

> I generally agree with Mick Keelty, he's doing a fantastic job. I see the same intelligence as he's seeing, and I disagree with him on this occasion. I think we're being attacked by al-Qaeda, J.I. and all other terrorists because of who we are and what we are, rather than where we've been or when we've been there.
>
> I consider that they've declared war on us, they've killed our sons and daughters, and now they're trying to divide us with words. It seems to me that they started this, and we're in it to the end, we are not going to be divided off from the few nations in the world that are taking a really strong stand.
>
> This is important stuff, and I believe that while Commissioner Keelty's point in a narrow sense – I can understand why he made it – I don't agree with it, and from my point of view let that not for any moment say that we should be more or less vigilant depending on what our foreign policy is.

We've got to be on the ball, we've got to have
people on the lookout all the time.

Mick Keelty was deeply affected by Cos' intervention.
Ironically, they have much in common: both are from
working-class, Catholic backgrounds, both followed a
family tradition into their respective careers; both
devoted husbands and fathers; both proud patriots;
both industrious, well-loved, compassionate leaders. They
had reached the top of their professions around the same
time and had worked together harmoniously for some
years. Each is known to like, respect and enjoy the other's
company. Keelty has always appreciated Cos' and Lynne's
hospitality to him and his wife Sue. Keelty would have
expected a reaction from the political sphere. He did not
expect Cos to join the queue of critics.

In the light of the unprecedented pressure being
brought to bear on him, Mick Keelty considered his
position. He briefly contemplated resigning. Instead, two
days after his original *Sunday* interview, he issued a media
statement 'clarifying' his remarks on the program.

It is important that I clarify my views on address-
ing the threat of terrorism, given the media
coverage of my comments on Sunday. I regret that
some of my words have been taken out of
context.

My strong view, which I have stated
previously, and which I repeated as recently as last
week in my Commonwealth Day address, is that

terrorism seeks to attack the liberal, democratic values that are central to our Australian way of life. This is the case no matter what our involvement in East Timor, Afghanistan and/or Iraq, as I have said before, we cannot allow terrorism to dictate national policy.

Pointedly, Mick Keelty did not withdraw his original statement, nor did he detail which of his words had been taken out of context. And he left it open for others to determine who had taken them out of context. Within hours Alexander Downer had changed his tune. 'He'll go down in history as one of the great police commissioners and I certainly have no intention of reflecting on him and his professionalism. He's an outstanding Australian.'

The following day, because the controversy had blown up against the background of a national police chiefs meeting attended by the Prime Minister, TV viewers were treated to an intriguing display of body language as Howard shook hands with his clearly wounded federal police chief.

Many observers have praised Keelty for his forbearance, pointing out that had he quit, it might have irreparably damaged relations between the government and the AFP, who backed Keelty to a man. In a subsequent profile on Keelty by Paul Daley in *The Bulletin* of 1 December 2004, a 'senior federal government source' is quoted in the issue.

It was potentially a massive problem made by Howard, Downer and [Philip] Ruddock. Nobody outside of the government or the cops really knew how serious it was: at a person-to-person level, we had to get them to trust us again. Once Keelty agreed to stay, there was not even a speed bump in our relations with him. With others, it has not been nearly so easy.

Later in the same article Keelty was quoted:

Well, there's a couple of things. One is that we've moved on a long way since then, but I think it was important that the community had confidence in me as a commissioner and also the AFP as an organisation, and a lot of the debate was around that issue of being independent. It was important to me that the organisation emerged from that with its integrity intact. And I think that's what happened.

It's a measure of both men that Cos and Mick Keelty have since mended fences and remain firm friends. Perhaps it's an illustration of the pressures of their jobs that the situation ever arose between them.

In June 2004 Cos and the Defence Department Secretary, Ric Smith, accepted the blame for providing the Government with inaccurate information on the abuse of prisoners in the Abu Ghraib prison. The situation arose after a Liberal backbencher called for both

Cos and Smith's resignations. Defence Minister Robert Hill claimed he'd been misled. Labor Opposition Defence Spokesman Senator Chris Evans countered by accusing the Government of forcing the defence heads to shoulder the blame.

> I think it's no coincidence that at 12.30 pm, just before the Prime Minister's to give a press conference, that Mr Smith reads a statement on behalf of himself and General Cosgrove that effectively absolves the Prime Minister.

The two defence heads were forced to retract their earlier claims that no Australian knew of prisoner abuse at the time it occurred. In fact, army legal officer Major George O'Kane had visited the Abu Ghraib prison several times, exposing the ADF to claims that it could have complained and perhaps prevented some of the subsequent ill treatment. Cos told the Seven Network's Chris Reason on the *Sunrise* program on 9 May 2004:

> I think it's a great tragedy. The thing I really see here is of course it's a dreadful sight. It's completely unacceptable and I know how mortified the vast majority of US armed forces and coalition troops who do behave properly will be at this which sort of attacks the reputation of all service men and women. It is a terrible thing and I know that the US is hunting down the perpetrators of this to get justice for the Iraqis who've

been treated badly. It just stigmatises everybody else.

Despite his ever-growing experience in politics, Cos learned that even the most innocent-seeming statement can be turned against him when the Leader of the Opposition, Mark Latham, used comments he made at a business breakfast to support his call for a withdrawal of troops by Christmas. (Cos had been reported in *The Age* on 1 July 2004 as saying that empowering Iraq to take responsibility for internal security and getting 'the number of troops — not least Americans — out of the country' would reduce terrorists attacks.)

Foreign Minister Alexander Downer came to Cos' defence, claiming Latham had 'verballed' him and that Cos was simply making the obvious point that once the Iraqis themselves were able to take control of their own security that would be preferable to foreigners having to do it.

The controversies rolled on when, in the build-up to the federal election, Prime Minister Howard used images of himself with Australian troops in Iraq in a pamphlet, entitled 'Staying the course in Iraq', that he mailed to voters in his Sydney electorate of Bennelong. The tactic drew a statement from Cos to the effect that images of ADF personnel should not be used for 'unmistakable political purposes'. The Prime Minister responded by noting that the photos were available on the ADF's website, that he had secured formal clearance for their use and that the Opposition had also used similar shots in seats that covered military bases. Some commentators made the time-honoured point that if you want to keep the military out of politics, you should keep politics out of the military. Cos felt he'd made his point and declined to respond further.

In December 2004 Cos was dealing with a storm in a teacup at Duntroon, where some cadets had tested positive to speed and ecstasy, when the Asian tsunami hit on Boxing Day. Initial reports had ten Australians dead and 5000 unaccounted for, among the countless thousands believed to have perished in what was recognised as one of the worst natural disasters in history. The ADF despatched aircraft and medical and relief teams immediately. The Indonesian military chief made contact with Cos and opened the way for the ADF and other Australian organisations to have unfettered access to assist. Cos oversaw the ADF's sustained response as it worked in concert with the Australian Federal Police and a myriad of other government and non-government agencies to bring medical aid and transport in the chaotic aftermath.

While Cos was dealing with the aftermath of the Boxing Day tsunami, as well as the patchwork of other military commitments, he was hit with news he'd been dreading. His son, Philip, who had been deployed without fanfare to Iraq, was injured in a roadside bomb blast while on duty in Baghdad in January 2005. Philip and his fellow soldiers had been guarding a diplomatic compound when the explosion happened. It was literally one of thousands occurring in the Iraqi war zone, but it was the only one Cos felt personally. Philip suffered temporary deafness and was flash-burned when the bomb detonated near the side of a building. Because of the excellent communications, Cos was informed and knew that despite his wounds, Philip had stayed on duty.

Cos was able to soften the blow with Lynne by telling her from the beginning that Philip had only been slightly hurt and was fine. He was even able to speak with Philip to reassure himself he was fine. It was a humbling experience, even to a hardened soldier.

Some months later, on 4 April 2005, Cos realised how lucky Philip was. He was advised that while HMAS *Kanimbla* was in the final stages of his work in helping with the tsunami recovery, one of its Sea King helicopters crashed on the Indonesian island of Nias, killing nine of the 11 crew members aboard. Cos spoke on their behalf.

> This is a shocking blow for all of them. They obviously will be very upset at losing their shipmates and other personnel, but just as they turn around and sail back to Sumatra, when they thought they were on their way home, I know here, as well as coping with this dreadful event, they'll get on with the mission of helping the people of Sumatra. It's in their nature, and I've got great confidence in them.

A subsequent formal inquiry revealed the likely cause of the crash was mechanical, with a faulty bolt breaking and sending the aircraft into a dive. The impact ignited butane gas containers, creating a devastating fire. Cos instigated an internal inquiry into the maintenance systems.

Things came full circle in the month before Cos completed his term as CDF when, in June 2005, the last Australian troops left East Timor. Cos spoke with pride as he expressed confidence that the East Timorese armed forces were ready to take control of the world's newest nation's security.

> Well, they're at a fledgling level, but they are never, I don't suppose, proposed to be very large, as would be, I suppose, appropriate for a small nation. But nonetheless, I think they're very proudly patriotic, and prepared to deter small groups of people who might wish, in some way, to breach the laws of Timor Leste.

One of Cos' final duties was to appear before a Senate Estimates Committee, during which he confirmed that the ADF had taken disciplinary action against some members of the SAS Patrol Kilo Three for an incident which saw 11 civilians killed in eastern Afghanistan after they had discovered what they mistakenly thought was an al-Qaeda stronghold. Cos told the committee:

> Some internal aspects of Patrol Kilo Three were investigated fully at the time and appropriate disciplinary action was initiated. For the protec-tion of our soldiers and their families the ADF

does not normally publicly discuss the details of internal investigations and any disciplinary actions taken. We treat these issues confidentially in order to allow the correct and appropriate application of military law.

In April, the government announced that Cos' replacement would be Air Marshal Angus Houston, who had clearly risen above his earlier scrape with the government during the inquiry into the children overboard affair. When he said there was no evidence to suggest that women and children had been thrown into the water Cos welcomed the appointment, calling Angus Houston a 'tremendous choice'.

On 1 July 2005, an emotional Cos took Lynne's hand as he drew the curtain on his 40 years in khaki at a parade outside the Russell Offices in Canberra. He left a very different position from the one he had assumed three years earlier. Cos brought the CDF into the public eye. Many observers pointed out you would have to go back to World War II and Thomas Blamey to find a general as well known, and to go perhaps as far back as World War I's General John Monash to find one held in such a high public regard.

But, in addition to Cos' undoubted flair for the limelight, the position also changed because of the different local and geopolitical environment in which it operated. Under the Howard Government the military in general – and Cos in particular – was elevated to the most prominent position it has ever occupied outside of the two world wars. Prime Minister Howard, President Bush and British Prime Minister Tony Blair all basked in the reflected glory of their military. Always well aware of the iconic position occupied by Australia's armed forces, Howard was able to astutely parlay it into a winning formula via East Timor and the 'war against terror'.

Some critics have suggested that Cos may have taken his eye off the ball to some extent in overall defence management, particularly in relation to forward planning on the large scale. They put this down to his lack of experience as the first CDF not to have served first as Vice-Chief since the position was first created back in 1980. They claim this led to a shift in power back to the individual services – the army, navy and air force, each with their own barrows to push – at the expense of an overall defence force approach. It's a question that will probably be answered in hindsight. As to Cos' position in the pantheon of our great military leaders, Professor David Horner puts it into perspective:

> General John Wilton ran the war in Vietnam for eight years. How long was Blamey head of the army in World War II? How many operations did Vasey command a division? Compare them with what Peter Cosgrove did. It's hard to put it in the same context or same breath because his were short commitments.
>
> But that shouldn't be seen as denigrating

Cosgrove. It's just a fact of modern-day command that if you're CDF you deal with a range of issues at the same time. He had the War against Terror going on as well as the illegal immigrants and he's developing the defence force, there's training to be done, the Solomons going on and peacekeepers around the world. The defence force is on operations the whole time that he was Chief Defence Force. That's modern day strategic command which is so different in its flavour to these commanders that commanded previous wars. So it's an unfair comparison.

David Horner sees Cos as operating in a different ballgame, management but also command, in the new post-Cold War environment. It's an era in which the commander works in a far more political environment than his equivalent in World War II. Today's military commitments are contentious and community expectations are quite different as to what is expected of a public institution or an individual in public office. The level of scrutiny is infinitely greater, as Professor Horner points out:

> How many times did General Wilton get interviewed about the Vietnam War? The press didn't expect him to do it, the government didn't expect the general to do it and the general didn't expect to do it. In fact, the government wouldn't let him do it.

As to claims that his position had been politicised, Cos was unequivocal in a chat to Chris Reason on the Seven Network's *Sunrise* program on 24 April 2005.

> It is rubbish. I've never been that way. I will stick up fiercely, ferociously, ceaselessly for the people that I command and the people who support the people I command. I will not let unanswered slurs impinge on their reputations. Their morale, their welfare is hugely important to me. If I see that I need to speak on those issues, I will. Where those issues have got a sort of political cloud around them, that obviously can create difficulties.
>
> But if I can assure your viewers that what I'm doing is sticking up for my people and those who support them, I can be judged and people can comment on me and people can attack me. It goes with the job.

THE ART OF
LEADERSHIP 11

There is a school of thought that believes leaders are born, not made. There are elements of Cos' life that support this theory but, equally, he has progressed through a system that has nurtured and developed his leadership abilities, and he has successfully tested them in the crucible of war. There is no question that he is a leader.

Perhaps leaders are an amalgam of their innate abilities and their training and experiences. Cos clearly had excellent leadership genes. He was born into a family steeped in military tradition. His father and his maternal grandfather were both outstanding role models and undoubtedly helped in his formulation of his future career. Very early, Cos showed signs of a natural propensity to take the lead – as he did when, at three and a half, he led his fellow kindy kids over the wall because of the bad lunches. As a schoolboy cadet, he naturally gravitated to command. He was awarded the Leadership Prize in the Waverley College Cadet Corps, a prize that was presented to him by the then Governor-General Lord de l'Isle. Cadet Cosgrove could not have guessed that within a decade he would serve as the aide de camp to one of his successors, Sir Paul Hasluck.

Cos is the first to admit that he had a long way to go to become a real leader when he began polishing his boots at Duntroon. If he had a field marshal's baton in his kitbag at that stage, it was packed right at the bottom. He has credited Duntroon as being 'perhaps the most critical influence in developing my leadership skills'.

Our instructors all had seen active service, and more than a couple had decorations for gallantry. There were some very distinguished soldiers on the staff, and we looked up to them, and modelled ourselves as leaders on those we admired. We were given every opportunity, in our barracks, on the sporting field, and in our training to develop our leadership potential. We were constantly being taught, observed and assessed.

We learned leadership in any number of ways from any number of teachers and mentors so that by the time we had graduated we had a clear vision of the sort of leader we wanted to be, and of the leadership style we would adopt.

The army recognised Cos' leadership potential. From his first posting as a humble lieutenant commanding an infantry platoon in Vietnam, the experience of leading in action and being responsible for the lives of 30 other young men as an untried 22-year-old left an indelible imprint on him.

> While Duntroon had gone a long way to preparing me for this role, the stark actuality of that responsibility was initially very confronting. An acute awareness of that responsibility has remained with me always.

After successfully emerging from his baptism of fire, he drew on a combination of ability, diligent application, determination and experience to see him through another eleven command positions right through to the top of the tree. By the time he was appointed Chief of the Defence Force, Cos was the most experienced commander in the force, as Professor David Horner attests:

> That is an absolutely unbelievable achievement. If you take it through platoon commander, company commander, battalion commander, brigade commander, Commandant of the Infantry Centre, Commandant at Duntroon, Commander of the 1st Division, Commander of the Joint Deployable Force, Commander of INTERFET, Land Commander, Chief of the Army, before he gets to CDF.

What is remarkable about Peter Cosgrove's career is the constant string of commands. The best way to learn how to be a commander is to be one – you're constantly commanding and you get comfortable with being a commander. You learn the techniques of how to manage your staff and how to lead a group of people and that continues as your command turns into a larger organisation.

Cos likes to relate the following tale, illustrating the vital importance of experience in becoming a successful leader.

A young aide asked of his retiring admiral how he too could rise to be a senior officer. The admiral told the young aide, 'Two words – right decisions.' The aide questioned the admiral, 'Well, how do I ensure that I make the right decisions?' The admiral said, 'One word – experience.' Again, the aide questioned, 'But how do I gain this experience?' The admiral replied, 'Two words – wrong decisions.'

He has often expounded publicly on the value of experience:

We all have at some time or other felt directly the effects of both the presence and the absence of leadership. Over the course of a long career and, most especially in East Timor, I had occasion to reflect that leadership for any of us is the sum of all the good and bad examples to which we individually have been witness. Both sorts of examples are useful.

In his accustomed style, Cos has been able to distil the job of the Chief of the Defence Force down to its basics.

> There's no particular magic in doing the job, it works basically the same way in every military command job: command, leadership, and management downwards; obedience and timely, accurate advice upwards; loyalty in both directions.

Cos has learned the vital difference between being a leader of men and women and simply managing them. He regularly quotes the words of one of his most admired leaders, the great World War II commander Field Marshal Sir William Slim, later Viscount Slim of Burma and Governor-General of Australia from 1953 to 1960, on the difference between the two.

> Leadership is of the spirit, compounded of personality and vision; its practice is an art. Management is of the mind, more a matter of accurate calculation, of statistics, of methods, timetables and routine; its practice is a science. Managers are necessary. Leaders are essential.

The Australian military has long espoused a simple, time-honoured approach to leadership: it should be 'fair, firm and friendly'. Clearly, it has not always succeeded in achieving those aims but they are catchwords Cos has consistently tried to live by and lead by.

According to the respected American psychoanalyst Erik Erikson, military commanders should possess two virtues:

> The first is purpose – the courage to envisage and pursue valued goals uninhibited by the defeat of infantile fantasies, by guilt and the foiling fear of punishment. The second is wisdom – a detached concern with life itself, in the face of death itself.

On the other hand, in *On the Psychology of Military Incompetence*, Norman Dixon considers the ideal military leader as:

> . . . one who manages to combine excellence as a task-specialist with an equal flair for the social or heroic aspects of leadership. Since the traits required for these two aspects of leadership are rather different, these so-called 'great man' leaders have been comparatively rare.

In more general terms, Dixon sees leadership as:

> . . . no more than exercising such an influence on others that they tend to act in concert towards

achieving a goal which they might not have achieved so readily had they been left to their own devices.

At a deeper and rather more important level, leadership depends upon a proper understanding of the needs and opinions of those one hopes to lead, and the context in which the leadership occurs. It also depends on good timing.

Cos has often said, 'I do my best and insist that people who work for me do the same.' This deceptively simple dictum has many benefits: it sets a clear, inspirational example; it engenders confidence because the team members know from the start that their leader is a contributor who will match them for effort; and it sets a framework within which the team members can comfortably work. This approach is also an example of leading from the front, something Cos has done since his time in Vietnam, although in those early days he was arguably a little too enthusiastic. While he has become more considered and more polished in the way he commands, he has always retained his desire to get on to the front foot – to be proactive rather than reactive. Perhaps this desire has also contributed to the positive energy Cos has always been able to generate in his leadership, a greatly underestimated ingredient in forming teams and leading them.

Above all, Cos has been, first and foremost, a soldier – an educated, articulate, adaptable soldier, certainly – and always a proud soldier. This has allowed him to travel through life secure in the knowledge that he is following a noble career, and has allowed him to work within a defined structure. He has always remained close to the digger and feels extremely comfortable in his presence. He believes that the digger maintains a sort of 'watching brief' on his officers, and that the officers must win and retain the respect of the digger. Further, that respect does not come automatically with a badge of rank, rather it must be individually won by performance and then retained by sustaining that performance.

> It's this sort of cheerful pressure on those who are appointed as leaders, which actually makes them much better. You know you don't prance around with a sort of conferred and acquiescently agreed mantle of authority as a leader in the army. You work all the time to establish and reaffirm your credibility and it can last just a few seconds if you come out with something dumb, if you miss the obvious point, if you're cranky for no reason, if you are dismissive of this sense of initiative. And you've also got to play within the boundaries because with that goes a tinge of irreverence which is the diggers, to some extent, always mildly pushing the envelope.

Top of his mind in all his operational commands has been the fundamental need to protect his troops at all costs. He underlined this to the students at the Higher Command and Staff College course as CDF in 2004:

As CDF I am conscious of my obligation to the Australian people and, if you like, to Australian parents. Indirectly, I prepare their sons and daughters to accomplish our missions, as safely and decisively as possible.

I acknowledge that war is a messy business and even the most seasoned professional may be killed in action. But I'll never be comfortable with the thought that young men and women might die because of a commander's 'damn fool decisions'. We're the professionals and we owe it to our people to avoid the arrogant stupidity that unfortunately litters the pages of military history.

For Cos, the single most important trait in a leader is integrity – based on honesty and trustworthiness. He sees it as forming the 'bedrock' of good leadership.

A belief in your integrity – as distinct from popularity – is what binds people to your ideas and vision. Without people believing in your integrity, even if your ideas are 'world beaters', others will not commit to them; or worse still they may simply even attempt to steal them.

The existence of a belief in you, and what you stand for, is enough to achieve the impossible; but without it the seemingly easy will be made more difficult. Staff may, over time, forgive a leader an absence of all other qualities – either singly or in combination, because given time and experience most qualities can be acquired or developed to a reasonable standard. The exception to this rule is integrity.

Another key ingredient in Cos' description of the ideal leader is compassion. It's one of the core traits long possessed by the Australian digger; one that has allowed him to seamlessly make the transition from warrior to peacekeeper, just as Cos and his team did in East Timor.

> In my experience leaders who exercise their authority in a humane and compassionate way are, in the main, the most successful over the long term. But, even more important are the positive and sustaining effects that such a style has on those who are led.

A characteristic that many observers have attributed to Cos is a 'calm assurance' or an 'unassuming self-confidence'. These are characteristics shared by many fine leaders, as Norman Dixon noted when he quoted R.W. Thompson writing that the great British General Bernard Montgomery 'had the knack of creating oases of serenity around himself'. Goronwy Rees, the Welsh academic and writer, remembered from his first meeting with Montgomery 'that air of calm and peace which he carried with him was so strong that after a moment my panic and alarm began to die away: it was something which one felt to be almost incongruous in a soldier.'

Cos has often spoken about similar leadership traits that he believes are desirable in leadership at all levels.

> I also strongly believe that a leader's self-confidence should manifest itself in a low-key manner if at all possible, while avoiding too the obverse trap of false self-modesty or deprecation.
>
> No Australian is happy to work for either a swaggering and arrogant leader, or for one who comes across as weak and consistently self-doubting. Leaders must be humble.

Cos has demonstrated an incisive understanding of the need not only to lead, but to be seen to be leading. In other words, to use whatever media is available, in all its forms, to present his message. Cos first showed his proficiency in using the media to deliver his message in East Timor. He did it by what he called his 'mum and dad' test where he targeted his key messages, put simply and directly, to the parents and families of his troops.

> I have learned over time not to be intimidated by the media, but rather to regard them simply as a medium which will allow me to present simple and clear messages – preferably without evasive or confusing 'officialese' – to ordinary and decent Australians . . . This target audience loathes spin doctoring and at the very least respects candour and directness, even where significant problems or shortfalls are concerned.

Cos took the view that he should speak directly to his target audience. He was not aiming his message at the media or the general audience they represented. He was not speaking to his political masters, his military superiors or other observers.

> I was talking to mums and dad because they wanted to know, every time they saw my ugly dial on the television, how is my kid going. I felt that that not only flavoured what I was trying to say but the actual words I used. I tried not to use a lot of military jargon which sort of puts up that barrier.
>
> Military leaders will need to be able to communicate not just with their soldiers, or their service men and women of all services, but with the constituency at home.

Cos has also spoken of the need for a leader to have the capacity to take the wide view: to be able to keep the 'big picture' in mind when planning and making decisions. He exemplified this graphically during his command in East Timor when he was able to balance the varied and often competing interests of his many stakeholders with his immediate and longer-term goals. Perhaps most impressively, he did this while having a clear picture of the kind of East Timor he wanted to leave after INTERFET; the kind of peace he wanted to secure and the legacy he wanted to be able to hand to the next generation. He had this in mind when deciding what kind of military responses he made to the militia threats in East Timor. He knew that the way in which INTERFET used force to achieve the peace could directly affect its quality and duration. The last thing he wanted was to secure some kind of temporary ceasefire that would flare up again as soon as his force departed.

In this respect, he has spoken about the need for a leader to trust his 'gut feelings' where he has to:

> Facts and hard information are always going to be better than instinct, but in the absence of the former, in the absence of facts and hard information, be prepared to go with instinct. Even with modern communications means, our decision-making in response to crises such as terrorist attacks must not be ponderous. There are inevitably inbuilt delays to our actions and our decision-making, therefore, must be slick, quick and accurate. Let the leader not be the obstacle.

Cos has consistently been a team player. He may see himself as the team's captain but he knows he cannot lead without the team. He referred to his command group in East Timor as his 'strap-on brain'. He has been at pains to give credit to those who served under him there for their contribution to the eventual success of the mission. This has been a running theme through his many commands and has resulted in an impressive reservoir of people who are proud to be counted as members of the various teams he had led.

Many of these team members give Cos credit for his foresight; his ability to think, plan and act one step ahead of the game. He explained his philosophy:

> By all means plan for likely strategic outcomes – but be prepared to vigorously refocus both yourself and your whole organisation onto undreamt of challenges – and opportunities – according to the actual cards dealt by fate.

This, of course, is only possible if you combine the big-picture view with the intellectual capacity to collect and process the knowledge and information necessary to accurately assess the likelihood of future events. Cos has developed the added skill of being able to adapt quickly and sensibly when his initial predictions aren't borne out by reality. His open mind is extremely valuable and prevents him from making too many decisions based on prejudice rather than fact. He has also highlighted the need to be able to act with dispatch and, on occasions, with firmness – even ruthlessness – when extraordinary situations dictate that. For example, if plans need to be changed immediately, then action must be swift and uncompromising.

> This vigorous refocusing may well require steel and even ruthlessness, what I would prefer to call hard driving on your part. Hence, again, the need for a strong character foundation in all leaders. The meek will not survive such a test.

Cos has pointed out that as Commander of INTERFET he gained a deeper insight into the importance of co-operation and the development and maintenance of personal relationships as vital components in achieving an overall goal. The negotiation and collaboration required to successfully work with the web of competing interests there – the multinational forces, the UN mission, the East Timorese, the many political masters as well as the Indonesians, the TNI and the militia across many disparate cultures – were vital in avoiding poten-tially perilous misunderstandings. 'I'm convinced that personal relationships and mutual respect encouraged people from my level down to "talk through" rather than "shoot through" issues.'

Cos has been consistent in his advice to others to resist the temptation to reach for the '10,000 mile screw-driver', to interfere or to micro-manage his team, unless you have a compelling reason. He sees it as a recipe for disaster, especially on big missions where things could end in, at best, inefficiency or, more likely, massive dis-ruption and frustration on both sides of the relationship.

He also advises leaders to share some of their hard-ships with their team because it will draw the team together and foster mutual loyalty. But, ultimately, the good leader must have the strength of character to take responsibility for the results of his decisions.

The best of leaders shoulder the blame and share the glory. I have never forgotten the dignity which a leader can instil in any man or woman in an instant through simple and genuine public expressions of gratitude and appreciation.

Like all successful leaders Cos has always been prepared to do his homework. From experience, he has developed great faith in the military approach to preparation and believes its planning culture has much that can be used in other areas of life.

> The essence here is determining clearly the precise outcomes you want to flow from your vision and to distil and refine them into an easily understood plan which is widely distributed.
>
> This methodical approach to planning need not be slow, but in my opinion the more formal and regular the planning process the more beneficial the outcomes: because of the clarity and structure which flow naturally from such forums.

Of course, the formal planning structure has to be balanced by a leader capable of swift and decisive adaptation when circumstances, as they almost always do, change.

Cos has won praise for mastering one of the most difficult aspects of leadership: balance – the ability to direct and guide with a light touch. 'I use a mantra to keep me on track: be careful what seeds you sow in seeking to bring about specific outcomes.'

The American soldier General George S. Patton Junior said, 'Moral courage is the most valuable and usually the most absent characteristic in men.' When he was tested in battle, Cos showed that he possessed rare physical courage. Perhaps even more admirably, he showed throughout his life the courage of his convictions, the moral courage that is at the core of all great leaders.

REFLECTIONS 12

For his last official duty on his last day as Chief of the Defence Force, Cos chose to lay a wreath on the tomb of the unknown Australian soldier in the Hall of Memory at the Australian War Memorial. Lynne and their three boys, Stephen, Philip and David, were by his side, as he completed a very personal symbol of his journey coming full circle.

Cos reverently laid the wreath at the foot of the beautiful marble slab on which is carved 'An Unknown Soldier killed in the war of 1914–1918'. He stood back and saluted. There was a deep personal significance in his gesture. The remains of the unknown soldier that rest in the shrine were exhumed from the Adelaide Cemetery on the Amiens Road, just outside the tiny French village of Villers-Bretonneux, where Cos' beloved grandfather Bob Henrys had fought in 1918. The unknown digger's remains had lain in a grave in the Adelaide Cemetery for 75 years before they were exhumed on 2 November 1993 and brought to Canberra to represent the 100,000 Australians who have died in wars.

Cos knew that Bob Henrys and his mates had helped to liberate Villers-Bretonneux during fierce fighting on Anzac Day 1918. To this day, the people of the village have maintained their gratitude to the Australian soldiers. The small primary school, named the Victoria Primary School in honour of the schoolchildren from the Australian state who donated their pennies to help rebuild it after the war, has a proud sign in English in its playground which reads: 'Do Not Forget Australia'.

★ ★ ★

Cos left the army with a lifetime of memories. One of the most satisfying was the sound of more than a thousand East Timorese chanting 'Viva Cosgrove!' on the docks at Dili as he prepared to board HMAS *Jervis Bay* to return home. One of his prized possessions is a scarf given to him by the UN Chief of Mission in East Timor Sergio de Mello – a traditional East Timorese scarf with the words INTERFET embroidered on one end and UNTAET on the other. It was a symbol of the impact that Cos and his men had on the future of the people of East Timor on the day that they left to return home. He was also presented with a Falintil uniform by Xanana Gusmao, a heartfelt gesture from one warrior to another and all the more significant because Gusmao had spent more than 20 years as a member of Falintil fighting for his country's independence.

It was one of many highlights in a career in which he can point to very few regrets, although one of those few was the way INTERFET had to leave while many East Timorese were yet to be repatriated from West Timor, where they had been transported during the final destructive backlash by the retreating Indonesian military prior to INTERFET's arrival.

Cos' worst moment as CDF came in the closing days of his command, on 2 April 2005, when he heard of the loss of nine of 11 crew members of one of HMAS *Kanimbla's* Sea King helicopters while helping with humanitarian work on the Indonesian island of Nias in the aftermath of the Asian tsunami.

> There is no doubt that the low point of my time as CDF was the sadness brought by the loss of our men and women in the Sea King tragedy – the numbers of people involved, and seeing their bereaved families and so many people without a loved-one. It was a terrible thing for the families, and a sad time for all men and women in the ADF, and as their leader I felt it.

Cos left a very different army from the one he joined in 1965. He watched it grow from the run-down remnants of the proud forces of World War II to rise again to become a respected and adaptable high-tech army, able to make its presence felt around the globe. He'd seen Australia's three services develop into an effective integrated joint force operating under a state-of-the-art network-centric warfare system. He'd seen the number of women in the forces almost double, the command structure revamped and the introduction of a wide range of sophisticated equipment and arms. He'd seen the forces, and their commanders, come under increasing scrutiny and had helped to develop their capacity and skills so they could serve in many countries and in an ever-increasing variety of tasks. During his time as the chief of these forces he'd overseen an extensive program of commitments from Afghanistan to the Solomon Islands, while providing on-call assistance to respond to terrorist attacks and natural disasters, like Bali and the Asian tsunami.

He left an army that had developed an extensive operational experience, particularly in joint-service situations acting in concert with other nations' forces. He oversaw the expansion of our Special Services capability, in all three services, and the creation of a new unit for dealing with chemical, biological and radiological warfare. On his watch, as Chief of the Army, the 9/11 terrorist attacks highlighted that the world had changed irreparably. As he liked to point out:

> The al-Qaeda attacks on New York and Washington were planned in internet chatrooms. The terrorists used email and mobile phones to exchange tactical information. They booked their seats online.

Cos also helped to guide our forces through the IT revolution and to give them the capacity to deal with the new threats that technology has thrown up:

> . . . a range of strategic effects within the grasp of individuals and small groups. These latter are agile and can mount lethal operations over strategic distances with relative ease and impunity. They may arrive in a business-class seat.

Cos remarked that he was troubled by the inequality and inequities that globalisation has highlighted. While the developed world has benefited greatly, the chasm between the haves and the have-nots continues to grow.

> There have always been haves and have-nots in the global community but the old inequities, real and perceived, between say the Peasant and the Prince, are now magnified, globalised and open to manipulation by those savvy in the use of culture and communications. Warfare, which is of course another, albeit extreme, form of political discourse, cannot stand and has not stood aloof from the influences of globalisation, the most pronounced strategic effect of which has been the collapse of time and space as planning factors. Geo-strategic space is no longer a reliable buffer and warning time often a luxurious irrelevance. The most physically proximate threats are not by definition the most dangerous.

Cos has reflected on Australia's commitment to Vietnam and, although he concedes it was a vital ingredient in his development as a soldier and a leader, he now believes our involvement was a mistake:

> On reflection I'd probably join the majority of Australians who thought in retrospect our involvement was not going to be successful. It was simply not going to work, and therefore with 20/20 hindsight we probably shouldn't have gone.
>
> ... At the time I'm very clear that the majority of Australians thought we should be there, and it was only as a very widespread public reaction started to persuade the government of the day that it was, and the alternative government, that we shouldn't be there, that the mood changed.
>
> The men and women who were there of course performed magnificently and, I think, felt a little abandoned by such a sharp swing in the public opinion, which was never really about them, but was about the overall political reasons why we were there in the first place.
>
> But I think that's just part of history and certainly at no stage did it decrease my commitment to serve because after all in the end the military does the lawful bidding of the government and always will.

Like a well-written script, Cos' career built to a crescendo over the final stages and ended in triumph.

He had come full circle in many ways: the tyro subaltern who saw active service in Vietnam was called on for a dramatic flourish in action in East Timor, and then rose to the pinnacle of his profession before retiring honourably. The front-line soldier had survived and flourished in the Byzantine corridors of Canberra.

Some critics have claimed that Cos' lack of experience in the political pressure-cooker in Canberra showed on a number of occasions: notably in his criticism of Mick Keelty and his lack of support for his former Intelligence Officer in Timor, Lieutenant Colonel Lance Collins. They also claim that under his stewardship the ADF began to show some signs of a return to the days where the three services looked after their own backyards at the expense of a concerted national approach.

But, countering these negatives are many columns of positives. To the vast majority of Australians Cos embodied the Australian soldier. When speaking at Cos' retirement ceremony, the Chief of the Army, Lieutenant General Peter Leahy, paid him a moving tribute, characterising him as 'a man for the times', a great communicator who possessed the personal qualities of an Australian leader.

> He knows his job, he is a student of military history, he knows his people . . . and above all he knows himself. He is confident, robust, inspirational and, most importantly in the Australian context, fair, firm and friendly.

He also pointed out that Cos cared about people and tried to help them.

> He is concerned about their personal develop-
> ment, their safety and security. He has been
> fiercely protective of those people he commands
> and we know that he has always stood up for us.

And he mentioned Cos' goodwill and sense of humour and bonhomie.

> [He] loves nothing more than a few beers and a
> good yarn. He has to be the champion storyteller
> in the army, and is at his most engaging and best
> among a crowd of soldiers telling yarns.

All entreaties for Cos to enter politics after his retirement – to his credit both sides tested the waters – have been rebuffed with a self-deprecating assurance that he was happy to make up for lost time with Lynne and his boys and to explore opportunities in the world of commerce. Perhaps this should not have been as surprising as it appears to have been to many observers. Soldiers – like teachers, nurses, police and many others who quietly serve the nation – are rarely motivated by a desire for wealth or the limelight (despite Cos' evident enjoyment of his time on the public stage).

Like many of his generation of baby boomers, Cos has no plans to hang up his slouch hat and go fishing, although cricket and rugby tests may feature prominently on his calendar. He plans to 're-wire' rather than retire and clearly he has an attractive package of experience, energy and a unique skill set that is clearly highly prized in business. Within a week of changing from his uniform into 'civvies' he was appointed to the board of Qantas and as a consultant to giant accountancy firm Deloitte Touche Tohmatsu. He was later appointed to Fosters' philanthropic body, the Fosters Grant Committee. He is in constant demand as an after-dinner and motivational speaker and commands a fee that he would have thought ridiculous during his time in khaki.

Indeed, less than a year after he retired Cos was called back to the public stage, the day after the Category 5 Cyclone Larry hit Far North Queensland on 20 March 2006. With more than 700 people left homeless and hundreds, perhaps thousands, of buildings destroyed, Cos swiftly accepted an invitation from Queensland Premier Peter Beattie to lead the task force coordinating the recovery. (Interestingly, this was another case of coming full circle for Cos as he'd helped out as an infantry company commander in the clean-up of Darwin in the aftermath of Cyclone Tracy in 1974.)

Peter Beattie had met Cos in East Timor and knew he was the man to help his state's north get back on its feet.

I know him and I respect him. He's a born leader and that's what we wanted in Innisfail . . . he has the capacity to get the very best out of everyone around him and what you see with him is what you'll get.

Just as he did in Dili, Cos moved into humble accommodation in Innisfail – in the centre of the devastation –
and rolled up his sleeves. He may have cut a substantially
more generous figure than he did in 1999, but he still
possessed the unmistakable bearing of a leader and his
common touch saw him win over the locals and help
draw them together to begin the long process of
recovery.

Now financially secure, thanks to his directorships, his
consultancies and his public speaking – not to mention a
lucrative book deal for his memoirs – Cos seems likely
to play similar roles in the future. His public-spirited
approach to life seems certain to draw him into the
arena, as does his 'Flying Cosgroves' gene, which lures
him towards the limelight.

Cos has repeatedly rebuffed suggestions of a stint at
Yarralumla but his unique amalgam of leadership and
communication skills and his ability to understand the
aspirations of the common Australian may yet see it
come to fruition.

GLOSSARY

ADF	Australian Defence Force
ADFCC	Australian Defence Force Command Centre
AFP	Australian Federal Police
Brigadier (Brig)	Officer commanding a brigade
CDF	Chief of the Defence Force
Chinook	Large transport helicopter
Claymore	('Clacker') Command-detonated 1.25-pound anti-personnel mine that fired 700 small steel balls in an outward arc
CO	Commanding Officer
Free Fire Zone	Area supposedly cleared of civilians in which artillery and air support could fire without prior clearance
IGIS	Inspector-General of Intelligence Security
INTERFET	International Force in East Timor
M16	5.56mm US-made automatic and semi-automatic assault rifle
M60	7.62mm US-made general-purpose machine gun
M79	US-made grenade launcher
MC	Military Cross

Medevac	Medical evacuation by any means, often by RAAF C-130 (Hercules) out of Vietnam to Australia
NCO	Non-commissioned officer
ODF	Operational Deployment Force
RAAF	Royal Australian Air Force
RAN	Royal Australian Navy
RAR	Royal Australian Regiment (infantry corps)
1RAR	1st Battalion, Royal Australian Regiment
9RAR	9th Battalion, Royal Australian Regiment
Recce	Reconnaissance
Reo	A reinforcement, new to the unit
Rules of Engagement	Rules for opening fire – generally required a hostile act to be, or about to be, committed, or positive identification of the enemy before reacting
SAS	Special Air Service, elite unit, mainly used for reconnaissance
SLR	7.62mm self-loading rifle, standard-issue automatic rifle for diggers in Vietnam
Squadron	Company-sized group, consisting of three sub-units, called 'troops'
TNI	Tentara Nasional Indonesia, the Indonesian Armed Forces

UNAMET	United Nations Mission in East Timor
UNMISET	United Nations Mission of Support in East Timor
UNTAET	United Nations Transitional Administration in East Timor
Vietcong	Vietnamese Communist, a name adopted by South Vietnamese communist guerrilla forces

TIMELINE: GENERAL PETER JOHN COSGROVE, AC, MC

FAMILY HISTORY

28 March 1806	Great-great-grandfather, Thomas Cosgrove, born in Killskerry, County Tyrone, Ireland (died 14 June 1864, Shellharbour, New South Wales)
10 August 1811	Great-great-grandmother, Maria (Mary) Blakely, born in County Tyrone, Ireland (died 3 August 1898, Moama, Victoria)
1831	Thomas Cosgrove married Mary Blakely in Dromore, Ireland Children: John Joseph Cosgrove (born 14 February 1831, died 6 June 1862) James (born 12 March 1833, died 10 November 1902) Thomas (born 8 February 1835, died 23 December 1902) Patrick Cosgrove (date of birth and death unknown)

William Irving Cosgrove (born
15 September 1842, died
19 November 1917)
Anne Maria (Nancy) Cosgrove,
m. Downey (born 4 August 1844,
died 31 January 1927)
Samuel Austin Cosgrove (born
22 June 1846, died date unknown)
Mary Jane Cosgrove (born
21 September 1849, died
5 February 1918)

8 February 1835	Great-grandfather, Thomas Cosgrove, born in Ireland (died 23 December 1902, Kalgoorlie, Western Australia)
1835	Great-grandmother, Ellen Condon, born in Bulli (died 2 May 1909)
18 December 1857	Thomas Cosgrove married Ellen Condon at Shellharbour
18 May 1867	Grandfather, John Nereus (Jack) Cosgrove, born in Shellharbour, New South Wales (died 8 August 1925)
21 September 1884	Grandmother, Madeleine Mary Stephanie Treacey, born in Victoria (died 2 August 1933)
11 January 1916	Father, John Cave Cosgrove, born (died 7 August 1985)
11 November 1918	Uncle, William Nicholas Pax Cosgrove, born (died 11 August 1943)

12 June 1920	Mother, Ellen Mary Henrys, born (died 18 April 1995)
2 July 1941	John Cosgrove enlists in AIF from regular army (as John Francis Cosgrove) at Paddington, Sydney
14 August 1942	John Cave Cosgrove marries Ellen Mary Henrys
20 August 1943	Sister, Stephanie Anne Cosgrove, born

CAREER HISTORY

28 July 1947	Peter John Cosgrove born
1950	Attends Peter Pan Kindergarten, Paddington, Sydney
1952 to 1958	Attends St Francis of Assisi Public School, Paddington
July 1961	Cosgrove family moves from Paddington to Waverley
1959 to 1964	Attends Waverley College, in 1964 appointed head of Waverley Cadets
January 1965	Enters the Royal Military College, Duntroon, Canberra
11 December 1968	Commissioned as Lieutenant after graduating from the Royal Military College
December 1968	Posted to the 1RAR and subsequently serves in Malaysia

3 August 1969	Arrives in Vietnam, joins Australian Reinforcement Unit at Nui Dat, Vietnam
20 August 1969	Posted to 9RAR, on Operation Neppabunna then underway (ran from 15 August to 15 September), Vietnam
30 September to 31 October 1969	Operation Jack, Vietnam
10 to 16 October 1969	Recommended for Military Cross for bravery
November 1970	Returns to Australia after service in Vietnam and posted to the Methods of Instruction Team
12 February 1971	Awarded Military Cross for service in Vietnam
1972	Appointed aide de camp to the Governor-General
1973	Posted as temporary captain to 5RAR as Company second-in-charge, then adjutant, then Company Commander Major by end of year
1975	Begins courting Lynne while company commander of 5-7RAR, Holsworthy, Sydney
17 December 1976	Marries Lynne Elizabeth Payne (born 11 February 1948) while posted as Instructor of Tactics at Infantry Centre, Singleton

9 March 1978	First son, Stephen John Cosgrove, born
1978	Attends Marine Corps Command and Staff College at Quantico, Virginia, United States
1979	Staff appointments in Sydney
17 October 1979	Second son, Philip William Cosgrove, born in Sydney
December 1979	Sent to Rhodesia as part of the Commonwealth Observers Team for transfer of power
1980	Appointed to Operational Deployment Force, Townsville, Queensland
20 December 1982	Third son, David Michael Cosgrove, born in Sydney
1983	Promoted to Lieutenant Colonel, Commanding Officer of 1st Battalion, Royal Australian Infantry
1984	Appointed Australian Army Exchange Instructor at the Army Staff College, Sandhurst, England
26 January 1985	Member of the Order of Australia (AM)
7 August 1985	John Cave Cosgrove dies
1987	Appointed Military Assistant to the Chief of the General Staff
1988 to 1991	Promoted to Colonel and becomes Director of Combat Development

1992 to 1993	Promoted to Brigadier and appointed as Commander of 6th Infantry Brigade
1994	Brigadier, National Defence College, India
18 April 1995	Ellen Mary Cosgrove dies
1995 to 1996	Takes command of the Australian Defence Warfare Centre, Williamstown
1997	Commandant of the Royal Military College, Duntroon, Canberra
March 1998	Major General, Commander of 1st Division and Deployable Joint Forces Headquarters, Brisbane
September 1999	Commander of INTERFET
February 2000	Appointed Land Commander
16 July 2000	Lieutenant General, appointed Chief of Army
25 March 2000	Companion of the Order of Australia (AC)
26 January 2001	Australian of the Year
4 July 2002	General, named Chief of the Defence Force
3 July 2005	Retires as Chief of the Defence Force and from the Australian Army
21 March 2006	Appointed Head of Cyclone Larry Task Force

LIST OF ILLUSTRATIONS

IN THE TEXT

(p. 1)
Peter Cosgrove in Vietnam, 1969
Courtesy of Graham Dugdale

(p. 33)
Peter Cosgrove at the Waverley College passing-out parade, 1964
Peter Collins' Collection

(p. 49)
John Nereus Cosgrove, 1910
Mitchell Library, State Library of New South Wales

(p. 61)
Staff Cadet Cosgrove on entry to Duntroon, 1965
RMC-A Archives

(p. 83)
Brigadier Peter Cosgrove, Commandant of RMC Duntroon, 1997
RMC-A Archives

(p. 111)
Major General Peter Cosgrove on the deck of HMAS *Jervis Bay*, ahead of his return to Australia, February 2000
© Newspix/Rob McColl

(p. 149)
Lieutenant General Peter Cosgrove named as the new
Chief of the Defence Force, May 2002
© Newspix/John Feder

(p. 169)
General Cosgrove in Iraq with Sergeant Michael Neil,
November 2003
Australian Government Department of Defence

(p. 187)
Lieutenant Colonel Lance Collins
© Newspix

(p. 207)
General Peter Cosgrove, 2003
© Newspix/Nathan Edwards

(p. 225)
General Peter Cosgrove
Australian Government Department of Defence

(p. 243)
General Peter Cosgrove at the tomb of the unknown
soldier, 2005
Australian War Memorial (PAIU2005/145.08)

BLACK AND WHITE SECTION

John Nereus Cosgrove in *Silks and Saddles* with Robert
MacKinnon, John Faulkner and Brownie Vernon
Courtesy of the National Film and Sound Archive

John and Bill Cosgrove as boys
Family collection

John Cosgrove and his wife, Ellen
Family collection

Leaving class of 1964, Waverley College
Peter Collins' Collection

Peter Cosgrove in the Third XV rugby team at
Duntroon, 1966
RMC-A Archives

Peter Cosgrove with Duntroon classmates Mike
McDermott and Bill Rolfe
Courtesy of Mike McDermott

Peter Cosgrove at a Duntroon fancy-dress ball with Mike
McDermott and a friend
Courtesy of Mike McDermott

Mike McDermott celebrates with Peter Cosgrove at
their graduation from RMC Duntroon, 1968
Courtesy of Mike McDermott

Lieutenant Peter Cosgrove at Nui Dat Base with a
fourteen-foot python, Vietnam, 1970
Australian War Memorial (JON/70/0367/VN)

Nui Dat Base from the air, 1970
Australian War Memorial (COM/69/0380/VN)

9RAR diggers plan an attack, Vietnam, 1969
Courtesy of Graham Dugdale

A soldier of 9RAR aims his rifle down a Vietcong
underground bunker, Vietnam, 1969
Australian War Memorial (EKN/69/0023/VN)

Bob Convery
Courtesy of Graham Dugdale

Captain Graham Dugdale
Courtesy of Graham Dugdale

Diggers from 9RAR head out on patrol, Vietnam,
1969
Courtesy of Graham Dugdale

The 9RAR sergeants' mess bar at Nui Dat
Courtesy of Graham Dugdale

Peter Cosgrove in B company, 9RAR's rugby team, Nui
Dat, 1969
Courtesy of Graham Dugdale

9RAR heads home from Vung Tau Harbour, Saigon
Courtesy of Graham Dugdale

COLOUR SECTION

Major General Peter Cosgrove
Tom Alberts
Oil on canvas
91.8 x 81.5 cm
Australian War Memorial (ART91505)

East Timorese separatist leader Xanana Gusmao and
Nobel Laureate José Ramos Horta at a press conference
in Jakarta, July 1999
© AFP Photo/Maya Vidon

Major General Peter Cosgrove and East Timor's Nobel Peace Laureate Bishop Carlos Belo, Dili, October 1999
© AFP Photo

Lieutenant General Peter Cosgrove with members of the multinational Peace Monitoring Group, East Timor, 2000
Australian War Memorial (PO3518.019)

Sergio de Mello and Major General Peter Cosgrove, February 2000
© Newspix/Rob McColl

Major General Peter Cosgrove reunited with his wife in Sydney, February 2000
© Newspix/News Ltd

INTERFET troops led by Major General Peter Cosgrove Sydney, April 2000
© Newspix/News Ltd

Major General Peter Cosgrove is invested by the Queen as a Companion of the Order of Australia, Military Division, at Government House in Canberra, March 2000
© Newspix/Megan Lewis

Chief of the Defence Force General Peter Cosgrove, Head of Mission Australian Representative Office Neil Mules and Australian National Commander Air Commodore Graham Bentley receive a convoy brief by 2nd Cavalry Regiment Australian Light Armoured Vehicle (ASLAV) Commander Lieutenant Ben Kelly, November 2003
Australian Government Department of Defence

General Cosgrove attends the Iraqi Coastal Defence
Force (ICDF) graduation ceremony at Umm Qasr,
September 2004
Australian Government Department of Defence

General Cosgrove meets members of the Iraqi Coastal
Defence Force at Umm Qasr, September 2004
Australian Government Department of Defence

General Cosgrove talks to troops at the Regional Assistance Mission, Solomon Islands (RAMSI), August 2003
Australian Government Department of Defence

Outgoing Chief of the Defence Force Peter Cosgrove at
Defence Headquarters in Canberra, 1 July 2005
© *The Sydney Morning Herald*/Penny Bradfield

Mick Keelty, the Commissioner for the Australian
Federal Police, at his headquarters in Canberra
© AFP Photos

General Cosgrove, leader of the Cyclone Larry Operation Recovery, March 2006
© Newspix/Cameron Laird

General Peter Cosgrove in Silkwood, near Innisfail,
after being appointed chief of the reconstruction effort,
March 2006
© Newspix/Safarik Eddie

BIBLIOGRAPHY

9th Battalion RAR, *Vietnam Tour of Duty*, self-published, 9RAR Association, Brisbane, 1992

Bean, C.E.W., *Anzac to Amiens*, Australian War Memorial, Canberra, 1948

Bergerud, E., *Touched with Fire*, Viking, New York, 1996

Carthew, N., *Voices From the Trenches*, New Holland, Sydney, 2002

Collins, L. and Reed, W, *Plunging Point: Intelligence Failures, Cover-ups and Consequences*, HarperCollins, Sydney, 2005

Coulthard-Clark, C., *The Encyclopaedia of Australia's Battles*, Allen & Unwin, Sydney, 1998

Dixon, N., *On the Psychology of Military Incompetence*, Jonathan Cape, London, 1988

Dwyer, V., *Duntroon: An Artist's Impression*, Lonsdale Gallery Press, Singleton, 2004

Erikson, E.H., *Childhood and Society*, Norton & Co, New York, 1963

Evans, G., *Slim as Military Commander*, Jonathan Cape, London, 1969

Fernandes, C., *Reluctant Saviour*, Scribe, Sydney, 2005

Fleming, J., *The Crest of the Wave: A History of Waverley College 1903–2003*, Allen & Unwin, Sydney, 2003

Galloway, J., *The Odd Couple*, University of Queensland Press, Brisbane, 2000

Grey, J., *A History of Australia at War*, Cambridge Press, Melbourne, 1999

Hanson, N., *The Unknown Soldier*, Doubleday, London, 2005

Horner, D., *The Commanders: Australian Military Leadership in the Twentieth Century*, Allen & Unwin, Sydney, 1984

Horner, D., *Crisis of Command,* ANU Press, Canberra, 1978

James, L., *Warrior Race*, Abacus, London, 2002

Keogh, E.G., *The South-West Pacific 1941–45*, Grayflower, Melbourne, 1965

King, P., *Australia's Vietnam*, Allen & Unwin, Melbourne, 1983

Laugesen, A., *Diggerspea: The Language of Australians at War*, Oxford University Press, Melbourne, 2005

Lennox, G., *Forged by War: Australians in Combat and Back Home*, Melbourne University Press, Melbourne, 2005

Lindsay, P., *The Spirit of The Digger*, Pan Macmillan, Sydney, 2003

McAuley, L., *The Battle of Long Tan*, Arrow Books, Sydney, 1986

McGregor, S., *No Need for Heroes*, Calm Books, Sydney, 1993

McPhedran, I., *The Amazing SAS: The Inside Story of Australia's Special Forces*, HarperCollins, Sydney, 2005

Manchester, W., *American Caesar*, Little, Brown & Co, New York, 1978

Miller, W.I., *The Mystery of Courage*, Harvard University Press, New York, 2000

Moise, E., *The A to Z of the Vietnam War*, Scarecrow Press, Maryland USA, 2005

Moore, D., *Duntroon: The Royal Military College of Australia 1911–2001*, RMC Canberra, 2001

Odgers, G., *Army Australia: An Illustrated History*, Child & Associates, Sydney, 1988

O'Neill, J.R., *The Flying Cosgroves*, self-published, 1996

Pemberton, G., *Vietnam Remembered*, New Holland, Sydney, 1990

Rintoul, S., *Ashes of Vietnam: Australian Voices*, Heinemann, Melbourne, 1987

Shepherd, B., *A War of Nerves*, Pimlico, London, 2000

Slim, W., *Courage and Other Broadcasts*, Cassell, London, 1957

Townsend, H., *Baby Boomers: Growing up in Australia in the 1940s, 50s and 60s*, Simon & Schuster, Sydney, 1988

SPEECHES BY GENERAL PETER COSGROVE

3 July 2002	Address at Chief of Defence Force Change of Command Ceremony
30 July 2002	Address to National Press Club, Canberra
11 November 2002	'Facing future challenges to future operations – an ADF perspective' – Challenges of Peace Operations

20 May 2003	Address to ADO Network-Centric Warfare Conference – 'Innovation, People, Partnerships: Continuous Modernisation in the ADF'
10 June 2003	Address to Sydney Institute – 'Good Partner, Neighbour and Ally: Reflections on Australian Defence'
22 August 2003	Address to the Group of Eight Universities HR/IR Conference – 'Leadership Challenges – Lessons Learnt'
25 August 2003	Address to Australian Institute of International Affairs – 'Flexibility in a Changing Environment'
11 September 2003	Address to Australian Disaster Conference – 'Communication and Leadership'
21 September 2003	Address to 'Roma Remembers – Heroes Avenue Ceremony'
10 October 2003	Address to Royal United Services Institute International Seminar – 'The Australian Defence Force in the New Millennium: Balancing the Present and Future Needs'
23 January 2004	Address – the Batman Oration, Melbourne
20 April 2004	Address to Joint Future Warfighting Conference

14 January 2004	Eulogy for late Lieutentant-General Sir Thomas Daly, St Mary's Cathedral, Sydney
6 February 2004	Address at Dedication of Memorial to Australian Prisoners of War, Ballarat
25 February 2004	Address to Rotary Club of Melbourne – The Angus Mitchell Oration – Today's ADF
16 March 2004	Transcript doorstep interview, Australian Theatre, Potts Point, Sydney
18 March 2004	Address to Security in Government Conference – Leadership in Times of Adversity
19 April 2004	Address at Launch of *Anzac: An Illustrated History 1914–1918*
28 April 2004	Address to IPAA Queensland Leadership Seminar Series – 'The Military in Modern Society'
11 November 2004	Address 'Leadership in an Interdependent World'
19 April 2004	Address to Launch *Just Soldiers* by Darryl Kelly
5 July 2004	Address to the Fulbright Symposium – 'A Military Perspective on Civil–Military Cooperation in the War against Terror'

16 July 2004	Address to Launch Duntroon, *An Artist's Impression* by Vivien Dwyer
17 September 2004	Address to launch *Monash: The Outsider Who Won a War* by Roland Perry
11 November 2004	Address to Higher Command and Staff Studies Course
6 December 2004	Address to 19th Annual National Prayer Breakfast
6 April 2005	Address to Launch *The Flight of the Scorpion*
12 April 2005	Address to the Sir Vernon Sturdee Seminar on Grand Strategy
14 April 2005	Address to Launch *The Somme* by Robin Prior and Trevor Wilson

ARTICLES

Barrowclough, N., 'Trouble in Spyland', *Good Weekend, The Sydney Morning Herald*, 5 April 2003

Harari, F., 'For Pete's Sake', *The Australian*, 28 February 2002

Knightley, P., 'Deadly Secrets', *The Bulletin*, 21 April 2004

Lague, D., 'Soldiers's Home Searched over Leak', *The Sydney Morning Herald*, 21 September 2000

Lloyd Parry, R., 'Australians Covered Up East Timor Terror Plot', *The Independent*, 15 March 2002

Lyons, J. 'Operation Backflip', *The Bulletin*, 3 August 1999

Lyons, J., 'Timor Dossier', *The Bulletin*, 12 October 1999

Lyons, J., 'Out of the Shadows', *The Bulletin*, 6 April 2004

Lyons, J., 'Rotten to the Corps', *The Bulletin*, 20 April 2004 (including 'The Toohey Inquiry – The Restricted Report')

Mac, P., 'Row over Defence Intelligence Grows', *The Guardian*, 5 May 2004

Ramsey, A., 'Not Exhaustive and Not Correct', *The Sydney Morning Herald*, 11 December 2004

KEY REPORTS AND INTERVIEWS

Australian Government Department of Foreign Affairs and Trade, 'Transnational Terrorism: The Threat to Australia', July 2004

Australian Senate Estimates Committee on Foreign Affairs, Defence and Trade, Reference Committee Hearings into Economic, Social and Political Conditions in East Timor, *Hansard*, 22 April 2004

Australian Senate, Foreign Affairs, Defence and Trade Reference Committee, 'Security Threats to Australians in South-East Asia', 2002

Australian Senate, Foreign Affairs, Defence and Trade Inquiry into the Effectiveness of Australia's Military Justice System, *Hansard*, 22 April 2004

Australian Senate, Foreign Affairs, Defence and Trade, *Hansard*: 4 June 2000, 4 June 2001, 20 June 2003, 25 September 2003, 27 November 2003

Blick, W.J., 'Report of the Inquiry on Behalf of the Inspector-General of Intelligence and Security into Concerns Raised About DIO by Lt. Col Lance Collins'

Carter Center Report, May 2003

Commission for Reception, Truth and Reconciliation in East Timor Report, 2005

Flood, P., 'Report of Inquiry into Australian Intelligence Agencies', July 2004

Interview HQ Training Command, General Peter John Cosgrove 235341, by Captain Martin Toohey, 11 June 2003

Interview with General Peter Cosgrove by Patrick Lindsay, Russell Offices, 12 November 2002

Interview with Lieutenant Colonel Lance Collins by Patrick Lindsay, 6 March 2006

Interview with Mr Bill Blick, Inspector-General Intelligence and Security by Captain Martin Toohey, 30 May 2003

Interview with Lieutenant Colonel Lance Collins by Captain Martin Toohey, HQ Training Command, 14 May 2003

Interview with Mr Walter Frank Lewincamp by Captain Martin Toohey, HQ Training Command, 13 June 2003

Interview with Professor David Horner by Patrick Lindsay, 29 March 2006

Interview with Lieutenant Colonel Lance Collins by Patrick Lindsay, 6 March 2006

Interviews with Colonel Mike McDermott by Patrick Lindsay, 1 March 2006

KEY PROGRAMS

Extract from the *AM*: 'Cosgrove prepares to leave East Timor' with Ginny Stein, first broadcast 19 February 2000 on ABC Radio National, reproduced by permission of the Australian Broadcasting Corporation and ABC Online. © 2000 ABC. All rights reserved. The full transcript is available at: http://www.abc.net.au/am/stories/s101631.htm

Extract from the *7:30 Report*: 'Howard calls for quick action on Iraq' with Kerry O'Brien, first broadcast 13 March 2003 on ABC TV, reproduced by permission of the Australian Broadcasting Corporation and ABC Online. © 2003 ABC. All rights reserved. The full transcript is available at: http://www.abc.net.au/7.30/content/2003/s806507.htm

Extract from the *7:30 Report*: 'Howard defends commitment of Australian troops' with Kerry O'Brien, first broadcast 18 March 2003 on ABC TV, reproduced by permission of the Australian Broadcasting Corporation and ABC Online. © 2003 ABC. All rights reserved. The full transcript is available at: http://www.abc.net.au/7.30/content/2003/s810039.htm

Extract from the *AM*: 'Vietnam veteran prepares to lead peacekeepers' with Sally Sara, first broadcast 15 September 1999 on ABC Radio National, reproduced by permission of the Australian Broadcasting Corporation and ABC Online. © 1999 ABC. All rights reserved. The full transcript is available at: http://www.abc.net.au/am/stories/s51940.htm

Extract from the *AM*: 'Howard to consider request to reveal intelligence files' with Matt Peacock, first broadcast 29 November 1999 on ABC Radio National, reproduced by permission of the Australian Broadcasting Corporation and ABC Online. © 1999 ABC. All rights reserved. The full transcript is available at: http://www.abc.net.au/am/stories/s69251.htm

Extract from the *AM*: 'Collins requests release of all intelligence investigation documents' with Matt Brown, first broadcast 20 April 2004 on ABC Radio National, reproduced by permission of the Australian Broadcasting Corporation and ABC Online. © 2004 ABC. All rights reserved. The full transcript is available at: http://www.abc.net.au/am/content/2004/s1090768.htm

Extract from the *PM*: 'Downer attempts to hose down Keelty controversy' with Mark Colvin, first broadcast on 16 March 2004 on ABC Radio National, reproduced by permission of the Australian Broadcasting Corporation and ABC Online. © 2004 ABC. All rights reserved. The full transcript is available at: http://www.abc.net.au/pm/content/2004/s1067158.htm

ABC TV, 'Dangerous Liaisons', *Australian Story*, 25 February 2002

ABC TV, 'Trust and Betrayal', *Four Corners*, 1 November 2004

ABC TV, interview with Peter Cosgrove, *Enough Rope*, 8 August 2005

ABC TV, interview with Xanana and Kirsty Sword Gusmao, *Enough Rope*, 18 July 2005

ABC TV, interview with José Ramos Horta, *Enough Rope*, 10 May 2005

ABC TV, Tony Jones' interview with Senator Robert Hill, *Lateline*, 14 April 2004

ABC Radio, 'Intelligence Wars: Behind the Lance Collins Affair', *Background Briefing*, 30 May 2004

Nine Network, Laurie Oakes' interview with Peter Cosgrove, *Sunday*, 4 August 2002

Nine Network, Laurie Oakes' interview with Senator Robert Hill, *Sunday*, 23 March 2003

Nine Network, Jana Wendt's interview with Mick Keelty, *Sunday*, 14 March 2004

Seven Network, Chris Reason's interview with Peter Cosgrove, *Sunrise*, 9 May 2004

Seven Network, Chris Reason's interview with Peter Cosgrove, *Sunrise*, 24 April 2005

INDEX

Abigail, General Peter, 100, 108, 109, 143, 151

Abu Ghraib prison, 215–17

Adelaide, 156

Afghanistan, 155, 174

Age, The, 149, 217

Agent Orange, 9

Albrechtsen, Janet, 201

Allen, Peter, 26–7

Annan, Kofi, 117

army, changes to, 101, 245–7

Army Newspaper, The, 31

Army Office, Director of Combat Development, 103

asylum seekers, 156, 161

Australian Defence Force
Bali bombings, 164
Command Centre, 142
contingency plans for East Timor crisis, 114–15
disciplinary action against SAS Patrol Kilo Three, 220
East Timor Policy Unit, 121
hierarchy and structure, 165–8
Incident Response Regiment, 178–9
Iraq, 172–9
Naval intra-net, 183
Network-Centric Warfare, 179, 182–4

Special Operations Command, expansion of, 178

Australian Defence Warfare Centre
Cosgrove Commandant of, 105–7
revision of written doctrines, 105–6

Australian Federal Police, 116, 164, 210

Australian Golf Club, 93

Australian, The, 157, 201, 202

Australian War Memorial, 243

Aznar, José Maria, 173

Bali bombings, 162–5, 210
ADF role, 164–5

Barrie, Admiral Chris, 142, 153, 155, 156, 157, 159, 161

bastardisation, 72
Fox Report, 72–3

battle fatigue, 15

Beattie, Peter, 251

Belcher, Florence Emily *see* Cosgrove, Florence Emily

Belo, Bishop Carlos, 118, 120, 137

Bien Hoa, Vietnam, 9

Blair, Prime Minister Tony, 173, 221

Blake, Murray, 25, 101

Blakely, Mary *see* Cosgrove, Mary

Blick, Bill, Inspector General of
Intelligence and Security, 195,
204
Blix, Hans, 171
Bridges, Major General Sir
William, 70
Brown, Colonel Roger, 198
Browne, Jason, 196
Bulletin, The, 60, 196, 197, 199, 214
Burma railway, 38
Bush, President George W., 170,
171, 221

Carnell, Ian, 204
inquiry into Lance Collins'
claims, 204
Carter Center, 118
Castellaw, Brigadier John, 134
Central Catholic Library,
Melbourne, 35
Changi, 38
Chaseling, Grant, 62, 65, 80
Chief of the Army *see* Cosgrove,
General Peter John
Chief of the Defence Force (CDF)
see Cosgrove, General Peter John
'children overboard' affair, 156,
157–8, 160, 221
Clark, Lieutenant Ivan, 8
Clinton, President Bill, 122, 169
Collins, Lieutenant Colonel Lance,
187–206
Brown Report, 198
Carnell inquiry, 204–5

complaint to Minister for
Defence, 195
East Timor intelligence officer
posting, 191–4
intelligence leaks, investigation
into, 194–5, 199
intelligence report on East
Timor, 189–90
'pro-Jakarta' lobby assertions,
190–1
'Redress of Grievance'
request, 195
relationship with Cosgrove,
190–1, 193, 203–4
Toohey report, 196–9
Tracey review, 197, 198, 200
views on Indonesian
occupation of East Timor,
188–9
combat, 'fog of battle', 21, 99
Condon, Ellen *see* Cosgrove,
Ellen
Condon, James, 51
Condon, Mary, 51
Convery, Bob, death of, 24
investigation of, 25–6
Cosgrove, Angela Madeline, 58
Cosgrove, David Michael (son), 96,
243
Cosgrove, Ellen (great-
grandmother), 51
Cosgrove, Ellen Mary (mother),
34, 35, 36, 42, 44
death, 105

INDEX

Cosgrove, Florence Emily, 58

Cosgrove, John Cave Francis
(father), 33–7, 42, 43–4, 59
   army career, 35, 36–7
   Bill's death, 40
   birth of Peter John, 34–5
   death, 102
   promotion, 76
   World War II service, 37

Cosgrove, John Nereus (Jack)
(grandfather), 35
   birth, 53
   death, 60
   education, 53–4
   film industry pioneer, 59–60
   'Flying Cosgroves', 53, 57, 252
   marriages, 58
   relationship with Madeline
      Treacey, 59
   theatrical career, 56–9

Cosgrove, General Peter John
   aide de camp (ADC) to
      Governor-General Hasluck,
      86–9, 226
   appointment to command
      INTERFET see International
      Force in East Timor
      (INTERFET)
   Australian of the Year, 152–3,
      158
   birth, 34–5
   birth of first child, Stephen, 94
   birth of second child, Philip, 95
   birth of third child, David, 96

Brigadier, promotion to, 104

British Army Staff College,
   posting, 101–2, 134

Bronte, move to, 44

Chief of the Army, 151–2,
   158
   Vietnam visit, 154

Chief of the Defence Force
   (CDF), 158–60, 161
   assessment of Cosgrove,
      222–3
   critics, 222
   last official duty, 243
   politics and, 166–8, 217–18,
      223, 250
   replacement, 221
   role as, 176–7, 229

Chief of the General Staff,
   Military Assistant to, 103

childhood, 40–4
   influences, 43–4

Commandant of Duntroon,
   107–9
   officer training, 107–8
   regulars and reserves,
      relationship, 108
   sport re-established, 107

communication skills, 47,
   90–1, 98, 105, 131, 236

Cyclone Larry, leader of
   clean-up taskforce 251–2

Infantry Centre, Singleton,
   Commandant of, 103, 169
   Director of, 103

Cosgrove, General Peter John *cont'd*
  Officer Instructor of Tactics
    posting, 93
  Irish ancestry, 49–50
  Land Commander, 151
  leadership, 31, 41, 47, 78, 97,
    98, 99, 225–41
    compassion, 234
    integrity, 233
    protection of troops, 233
    respect, 232
    self-confidence, 234–5
  Lieutenant Colonel,
    promotion to, 96
  Lieutenant, 80
  Major, promotion to, 92
  Major General, promotion to,
    109
  marriage of parents, 35, 36
  marriage to Lynne, 92–3
  Methods of Instruction Team,
    posting with, 83
  physical abilities, 45, 65–6,
    73–4, 77
  religious education, 42
  retirement, 250–2
  Royal Military College,
    Duntroon, 61, 77–9, 80,
    107–9
    graduation from, 2, 80
    influence of instructors,
      77–8 *see also* Royal
      Military College,
      Duntroon

secondary education, 44–8
  cadet corps, 45–8
  Leadership Prize, 226
  Leaving Certificate, 48
  sport, 45
  6th Brigade, command of,
    104
Cosgrove, Lynne (née Payne),
  92–6, 100, 102, 150–1, 152,
  154–5, 162, 219, 221, 243, 250
Cosgrove, Mary (great-great-
  grandmother), 50
Cosgrove, Mildred, 58
Cosgrove, Noël, 58, 59
Cosgrove, Philip William (son), 95,
  150, 218–19, 243
Cosgrove, Stephanie (sister), 34, 40,
  41
  birth, 37
Cosgrove, Stephen John (son), 94,
  150, 243
Cosgrove, Thomas (great-great-
  grandfather), 51
  army service, 49
  emigration to Australia, 50
Cosgrove, Thomas Junior (great-
  grandfather), 50, 51
  death, 56
  marriage to Ellen, 51
  move to Sydney, 52
  prosperity, 51–3
  Western Australia, move to,
    55–6
Cosgrove, Tom, 53, 57

Cosgrove, Will, 53, 55, 57
  Cosgrove Musical Comedy
    Company, 57–8
Cosgrove, William Nicholas Pax
  (Bill) (uncle), 35, 59
    daughter, Madeleine, 39
    wife, Dorothy, 39
    World War II service and
      death, 38–40
Crown Street Women's Hospital,
  Sydney, 34
Cultana, South Australia, 2
Cyclone Larry, 251–2

Daley, Paul, 214
Dat Do, Vietnam, 4
Dauth, John, 112
de Mello, Sergio Viera, 144, 145,
  244
Defence Intelligence Organisation
  (DIO), 189
    Cosgrove defence of, 201–3
    role in East Timor, 192–4
Defence Signals Directorate, 113
Delta Company 5RAR, Cosgrove
  second-in-command posting,
  89, 90
    amalgamation with 7RAR, 92
    Cosgrove appointment as
      commander, 92
Denton, Andrew, 92
diggers
    Cosgrove relationship with,
      177–8

spirit of, 103–4
  Vietnam, 22–3
Diggers' Rest Fire Support Patrol
  Base, Vietnam, 9
Dixon, Norman, 230, 234
Downer, Alexander, 116, 211, 214,
  217
Dugdale, Captain Graham, 8, 11,
  17, 19, 25, 26
Dunn, General Peter, 80
Duntroon see Royal Military
  College, Duntroon
Dyer, Jack, 39, 40

East Timor, 113, 187, 188
    ADF contingency plans,
      114–15
    assistance to Australian diggers
      in World War II, 135, 137
    Australian troops leave, 220
    Carter Center report on
      violence, 118–19
    difficulties faced by
      INTERFET, 128–32
    evacuation, 119
    Falintil, 121, 245
    Fretilin, 121
    history, 134–7
    INTERFET troops, 124–134
    invasion by Indonesia, 1975,
      135
    Kopassus, role of, 114
    massacre at Liquica, 115
    media presence, 127–8

East Timor *cont'd*
  militias, 113, 115–19, 127, 133
  murder and torture, evidence
    of, 132, 139
  Operation Concord *see*
    Operation Concord (East
    Timor)
  Operation Faber *see* Operation
    Faber (East Timor)
  Operation Spitfire *see*
    Operation Spitfire (East
    Timor)
  reduction of Indonesian
    military presence, 144
  referendum, 112, 115, 117
  refugees, 117, 120, 139, 145
  Tentara Nasional Indonesia
    (TNI), role of, 113, 121
  UN-brokered agreement,
    115–16
  UN compound, 117, 120
  UNAMET, 120, 144
  UN's unarmed civilian
    policing group (Civpol), 116
  violence after election, 117
  West Timor, border with,
    130–1, 141
East Timor Commission for
  Reception, Truth and
  Reconciliation, 117, 135
8th Battalion RAR, 24
Eiler, Charlie, 3
Erikson, Erik, 230
Evans, Senator Chris, 216

Falintil, 121
family military background, 38,
  49
federal election 2001, 156–7
Fernandes, Major Clinton, 120–1,
  194
1st Battalion Royal Australian
  Regiment, command of, 96–101
    Operational Deployment
     Force (ODF), 96, 101
    sporting competitions, 98
    training exercises, 97–8
first combat action in Vietnam,
  11–15
1st Division and Deployable Joint
  Force (DJS) Headquarters,
  Cosgrove Commander of, 109,
  114
    appointment of Collins, 190
5 Platoon B Company 9RAR,
  command of, 4–27
    radio call sign 'Sunray
    Two-Two', 11
Fox, Supreme Court Justice R.W.,
  72
'fragging', 24
Fretilin, 121

Gillespie, General Ken, 182
globalisation, 247
Gorton, John, 85, 87
Graham, Midge, 7
Great Depression, 35
Gusmao, Xanana, 145–6, 244–5

Habibie, President B.J., 112, 115, 122

Hallam, Johnny, 7

Hasluck, Governor-General Paul Meernaa Caedwalla, 86–9, 226

Hat Dich, Vietnam, 9

Henrys, Bob (maternal grandfather), 34, 40, 43, 244
death, 75
World War I service, 37–8
World War II service, 38

Henrys, Ellen Mary see Cosgrove, Ellen

Henrys, Ernie, 38

Hickling, Frank, 101

Hill, Senator Robert, 197–8, 204, 216

Hogan, Colonel Gary, 199

Holsworthy, Sydney, 92, 96

Holt, Harold, 87

Horner, Professor David, 129, 146, 166, 167, 180, 222, 227

Horta, José Ramos, 137, 144, 145

Houston, Air Marshal Angus, 160, 221

Howard, Prime Minister John, 112, 122, 140, 156, 173–4, 180, 210–11, 217, 221

Huntley, John, 101

Hussein, Saddam, 169, 171, 173
ultimatum by Bush, 173
UN Resolutions regarding weapons of mass destruction, 169, 170, 172, 173

Indian National Defence College, 104–5

Indonesia, 112
'independence' ballot for East Timor, 112–13
invasion of East Timor 1975, 135–7
Kopassus, 114, 209
military role in East Timor, 113–14
role in violence in East Timor, 120–1
Tentara Nasional Indonesia (TNI), 113
UN-brokered agreement, 115–16

Infantry Centre, Singleton, 93, 103, 169

intelligence leaks, 194, 199

International Force in East Timor (INTERFET), 122
aims, 123
ambush by TNI troops, 133
command appointment, 123
composition, 124
deployment of troops to East Timor, 124–6
difficulties faced by, 128–32
effects, 144, 147
farewell ceremony, 145–6
intelligence database TOPIC, interrupted access to, 141, 192, 201–2
lack of preparation, 124

International Force in East Timor
cont'd
militias and, 133
murder and torture, evidence
of, 132
reason for success, 148
International Monetary Fund
(IMF), 122
Iraq, 169
Abu Ghraib prison, 215–17
commitment of Australian
forces, 173, 179–80
Network-Centric Warfare
role, 182–4
Operation Falconer *see*
Operation Falconer
preparations for action against,
170–3
reduction of Australian troop
commitment, 180
Israel, 174

Jenkins, Mervyn, 188, 195
Jeudwine, Wing Commander John,
39
Joint Intelligence Organisation, 188
Indonesian desk, 188
Joint Services Staff College, 103
Jones, Tony, 197

Kanimbla, 171, 219
inoculation controversy, 171
Sea King helicopter crash,
219, 245

Keating, General Michael, 100, 108,
109, 142, 143–4, 151, 153, 193
Keelty, AFP Commissioner Mick,
116, 164, 165, 197, 209–15
increased threat to Australia
through Iraq, 209–14
relationship with Cosgrove,
212–13, 215
Knightley, Phillip, 206
Kokoda Track, 36, 108
Kuwait, invasion of, 169
Desert Shield, 169
Desert Storm, 169

Land Warfare Centre, Canungra, 2
Lateline, 197
Latham, Mark, 217
Lavarack Barracks, 208
leadership *see* Cosgrove, General
Peter John
Leahy, Peter, 151, 158
tribute to Cosgrove, 249–50
Leigh Creek, South Australia, 2
Lewincamp, Frank, 193, 196, 205
Lewis, Brigadier Duncan, 156
Linnell, Garry, 16
Long Tan, Vietnam, 154
Lynch, Phillip, 72
Lyons, John, 196

McDermott, Mike, 3, 25, 65, 69,
73, 74, 75, 77, 79, 80, 93
McMahon, William, 85, 87
McNarn, Brigadier Maurie, 184

INDEX

Madrid train bombing, 209, 211

Mayer, Private Garry, 1–2, 6–12, 18

media, 127–8, 142, 207–8, 223, 235

Military Cross (MC), 16–19, 85–6
   recommendation report for
     Cosgrove, 20–1

Military Police, 25

mine warfare training, 3

Monash, General John, 221

Moore, John, 143, 149–50

Morrison, Lieutenant Colonel
   Alby, 2, 19, 25, 26

Muggleton, Regimental Sergeant
   Major, 64

Nagle, George, 7

Newman, Colonel Kevin, 89, 90, 91

Newton, Maxwell, 72

9th Battalion Royal Australian
   Regiment (9RAR), 2
   5 Platoon B Company, 2, 4–27

Nui Dat, Vietnam, 9, 21–2, 23
   diggers rest and recreation
     area, 22
   routine, 23

Nunnerley, Mildred see Cosgrove,
   Mildred

O'Brien, General Michael, 80

O'Kane, Major George, 216

Operation Anode (Solomon
   Islands), 185, 186

Operation Bali Assist, 185

Operation Belisi (Bougainville),
   185

Operation Catalyst (Iraq), 185, 186

Operation Citadel (East Timor),
   185

Operation Concord (East Timor),
   116

Operation Dark Moon (Australia),
   90

Operation Faber (East Timor), 116

Operation Falconer (Iraq), 174–5

Operation Jack (Vietnam), 9, 19,
   23, 85

Operation Neppabunna
   (Vietnam), 4, 8

Operation Slipper (Afghanistan),
   155

Operation Spitfire (East Timor),
   119–20

Operation Warden (East Timor),
   121
   initial international response,
     121–2

Order of Australia (AM), 102

Pacific Armies Chiefs Conference,
   154

Paddington, Sydney, 40

Payne, Lynne Elizabeth see
   Cosgrove, Lynne

Persian Gulf, 171

Peter Pan Kindergarten, Sydney, 41

Phu My, Vietnam, 21

Phuoc Tuy Province, Vietnam, 21

Portugal, 115
Powell, Colin, 171

Reason, Chris, 216, 223
regimental system, value of, 99–100
Reith, Peter, 156
Rhodesia, 96
Richmond Tigers, 38, 39, 40
Royal Marines, 176
Royal Military College, Duntroon,
    2, 46, 61–81, 101, 152, 218
    bastardisation, 72–3, 75
    bush orientation camp, 65
    college motto, 81
    Cosgrove Commandant of,
        107–9
    Fourth Class Cadets, 64–5,
        67–71
    hazing, 67–72
    influence of instructors on
        Cosgrove, 77–8
    Kokoda Company, 66
    Lanyard Parade, 71
    leadership skills, 226
    'screed test, the', 70
    Seven Wonders of Duntroon,
        70–1
    sport, 76–7
    University of New South
        Wales, link with, 72
Ruddock, Philip, 156, 211

St Francis of Assisi Primary
    School, Sydney, 42

St Joseph's College, Sydney, 54
St Mary's School, Sydney, 53–4
Sanders, Colin, 80
Sanderson, General John, 101, 123
SAS troops, 155, 174–6
Senate Estimates Committee, 220
September 11, 2001, 155, 246
Shalders, Vice-Admiral Russ, 158
Shoalwater Bay, Queensland, 2
Shore, Harvey, 67
Sindonis, Arthur, 211
Singapore, fall of, 39
Slim, Field Marshal Sir William,
    229
Smith, Ric, 166, 201, 202, 205, 215
Smith, Terry, 92, 93
Songkitti, General, 134
Sparrow Force, 134
Stephenson, Ivan, 16
strategic planning abilities, 106,
    123, 181
        Network-Centric Warfare,
            179, 182–4
Sunday, 209, 213
Sunrise, 216, 223
Sydney
    growth of, 52
    horseracing, 53, 54
    theatre, 54–5
Sydney Morning Herald, The, 194,
    206

'tall poppy' syndrome, 153
terrorism, 155, 246

ADF response, 178–9
Toohey, Captain Martin, 190,
    196–7, 199–200, 205
    report on Collins' claims,
        196–9, 202
Townsville, 96, 208
Tracey, Richard, 197, 200
Treacey, Madeleine (grandmother),
    35, 59, 60
Trocadero, 35
tsunami, 218, 219

Umm Qasr port, Iraq, 176
United Nations (UN), 115
    condemnation of Indonesian
        invasion of East Timor in
        1975, 136
    General Assembly, 122
    Mission in East Timor
        (UNAMET), 120, 144
    Secretary General Kofi Annan,
        117
    Security Council, 122, 169,
        174–5
    unarmed civilian policing
        group (Civpol), 116
    weapons inspectors, 169, 172
United States, action against Iraq,
    172
US Marine Corps Staff College,
    Quantico, posting, 94–5
University of New South Wales, 72

Vickery, Brian, 18

Victoria Barracks, Paddington, 35,
    96, 151
Vietcong
    bunkers, 10, 11, 16
    Main Force units, 9
Vietnam, 248
    anti-war movement, 84
    lessons learned, 27–31, 83–4,
        99
    withdrawal of Australian
        troops, 85
Vung Tau, Vietnam, 2, 26

Walsh, Gerald, 72
Waverley College, Sydney, 44–8,
    93
weapons of mass destruction, 169,
    170–3
    existence of, 172, 185
West Timor, 113, 117, 118, 121,
    139, 145
    border with East Timor,
        130–1, 141
    refugees, 145
Whitlam, Gough, 85, 86–7, 89
Williamson, James Cassius (JC),
    54–5
Wollongong, 51
Woodside, Adelaide, 2
Woolcott, Richard, 135

Yudhoyono, President Susilo
    Bambang, 117